SEW A BEAUTIFUL
HOME

Sally Cowan

Krause Publications
700 East State St., Iola, WI 54990-0001
Telephone 715-445-2214
www.krause.com

Please call or write for our free catalog of publications. Our toll-free number to place an order or obtain a free catalog is 800-258-0929 or please use our regular business telephone 715-445-2214 for editorial comment and further information.

Library of Congress Catalog Number: 99-64192

ISBN: 0-87341-804-2

Printed in the United States of America

The following trademarked or registered company and product names appear in the book:

American Girls™, baby lock®, baby lock Ese2®, Creative Dolls®, Dauphine™, Elastic Wizard™, Fasturn®, Fiskars® Softgrip®, Keeping You In Stitches®, Ribbon Wizard™, ShortCut® Snip, UltraSuede®, Velcro®.

Dedication

*This book is dedicated to my
parents, who believe I am
capable of doing anything; my
husband, Cary, who believes I am
capable of doing almost
anything; my brother, who
painstakingly took the photographs
and wonders if I'm
capable at all; and my cat,
Terry, who knows I am capable
of using a can opener, the only thing
that really counts.*

Acknowledgments

Top: Robin's design class busy working on their individual projects.
Middle: They even let me take part in their class. Here I'm doing a little ironing for Ginger.
Bottom: My brother, George McHendry, enjoying a well deserved break from the photo shoot.

To the following I extend my thanks for assistance throughout this project: Kelley Yarbrough Interior Design, Inc. St. Augustine, Florida, and those who work there: Jennifer Bean, American Society of Interior; Kelley Yarbrough, licensed interior designer; Tiffany Eubank Parker, designer; Anthony Fortunato, designer; and Julie Schenholm, business manager.

My appreciation to Robin McCallister, owner of Robin McCallister Designs in Jacksonville and design instructor at Florida College. Also to all her students who took part in this project - their hands truly mattered: E.H. Andrews, Phyllis Newton, Susan Weeks, Ginger Wallace, Barbara Lawrence, Richard Murphy, Christie Brown, Laura Simmons, Althea Mikell, Karen Edwards-Baggs, Barbara Armstrong, Mary Ellen DeMarco, Judy Carter, Josephine Bell, and Susan Weeks.

To JoAnn, Etc. in Jacksonville for kindly providing a location to photograph props and supplies and share pertinent information.

Special thanks to those who made it possible to enter The Oldest House in St. Augustine and the Castillo de San Marcos in St. Augustine.

Another thanks to The Greens Condominiums, St. Augustine Shores, where we were able to photograph one room and change it into six different styles.

My heartfelt thanks to baby lock, Tacony Corp., Fenton, Missouri, and Donna Saylers, "the fur lady."

Without my computer specialist Stacy Layman, this book would have been impossible.

Locations of Florida homes that opened their doors for photography include San Marco, Deerwood, Jacksonville Beach, Atlantic Beach, St. Augustine, Island Hammock, and Hastings

All photographs are by my brother, George McHendry, of Broomfield, Colorado.

Many thanks to my artist, Bob Layman, who holds a Bachelor of Fine Arts from the University of Washington, Seattle, who also cooks and constructs "things" in the St. Augustine area.

Preface

To sew a beautiful home requires researching and asking questions of those around us who know about the field of interior design. Perhaps a local shop owner or a friend who understands styles and colors would be a good source. I was fortunate to surround myself with two components that made my job just a little easier. The first was an interior design studio who had access to many beautiful houses. The second was a designer who teaches and works in the field - in the real world. Getting insight into how the "pros" do it is just one way to learn new ideas and professional tips. The fun of designing includes the fun of making friends along the way. I think it is meaningful to find out what brings a person to their chosen field, so I asked these individuals to share with you their love of design.

FROM THE DESIGN STUDIO

by Kelley Yarbrough and Jennifer Bean
Kelley Yarbrough Interior Design, Inc., St. Augustine

Our interior design studio is dependent upon the talents of our creative staff members, the talents of the many craftspeople who comprise the work force of our work rooms, and the talents of our outside sub-contractors and suppliers. Each member of our staff establishes an individual relationship with our clients during the time required to complete the design. A designer must have natural creative abilities, a dose of business knowledge, a dash of psychology, and knowledge of the tremendous number of resources available.

Working with Sally and George on the photo shoot for this book was a learning experience for everyone involved. After several days, they learned what we do for our clients and we learned a lot about the technical side of photography and lighting. The end result of all this hard work was the starting point of the book. Special thanks to our clients who allowed us to invade and photograph their homes.

LET THIS BOOK INSPIRE YOU

by Robin McCallister, Robin McCallister Designs, St. Augustine

My love affair with sewing began when I was a child. I remember watching over my mother's shoulder as she made a new dress for me or my sister or some new doll clothes for my Barbie. I am thankful that she passed that skill on to me. I am also thankful for those patient home economics teachers in junior high and high school.

The transition from clothing construction to home decorating came years later. The purchase of a new home sparked my desire to learn how to make my own window treatments. I purchased fabric from a local decorator fabric store, read books like this one, found a class at the local community college, and I was off and running. Sewing for the home became my passion and began to grow into more than that. After taking some classes and improving my skills, I began teaching one of the window treatment design classes at that same community college. And in 1999, after 20 years of working in the business world and seven years of making window treatments part-time, it became my full-time career. I am very blessed that my hobby became a business that I thoroughly enjoy.

I hope this book will be a great reference guide and inspire you to try a project on your own. Be encouraged that you can take those sewing skills, whether they be newly learned or a little dusty, and create something wonderful to make your home the reflection of you.

Top: Kelley and Jennifer were instrumental in bringing Sally's ideas to fruition and helped coordinate the photo shoot locations.
Bottom: Robin McCallister hard at work.

Happy Sewing!

Table of Contents

Introduction

Before I started writing this book, I flipped through dozens of books on home decorating. It concerned me that while many books showed hundreds of ideas, most didn't acknowledge that there are basic techniques that must be understood to accomplish most home decorating projects. In most books, if the basic techniques were mentioned at all, they were quickly brushed over.

This book is arranged so that the techniques, tools, definitions, measurements, hand stitches, and machine stitches are first and foremost. Once you become familiar with these, you'll move on to chapters filled with step-by-step projects and decorating ideas that take the basics a step further (and further). The sewing techniques you learn by finishing one project can be easily applied to another project. The idea is to develop growth in your home decorating experience.

If you're not an experienced sewer, don't worry. You won't be left out or feel overwhelmed. There is something for everyone here. To inspire your creativity, the projects are illustrated with drawings as well as color photos.

I hope that a total understanding of the basics, along with the many tips and ideas presented, will encourage you to become the "home decorator of the year." As an extra bonus, I added a pinch of humor. With all these techniques under your belt, you will be able to truly make your house your home. I do hope you have fun doing it.

Your home is where your heart is. Your home is where you can find peace, solitude, love, privacy, and safety. But your home is also a place you open to others.

A home has a way of taking on your personality. The choices you make as you decorate give your friends and visitors a picture of who you are. I realize there are times when this might not be a fair barometer because the grandchildren may have just dropped by or your wet dog may have just bounded across your beige carpet, but as a rule, your home reflects *you* - grandchildren, pets, and all.

So what does that mean? It means that only *you and your family* should make decorating decisions. This book takes into account a wide range of choices. Perhaps you want to add a special touch in the bathroom or some texture or color to brighten up the bedroom. Or you may want to redecorate the whole house. The projects in this book aren't just for mansions - I would like everyone who wants to improve the appearance of any feature of their home to feel a part of this book.

You will find home decorating solutions for the obvious areas - bedrooms, kitchens, bathrooms - but you will also find decorating ideas for special and challenging areas like hallways, corners, attics and lofts, home offices, RVs, and even your pet's corner (after all, a happy pet is a loyal pet!).

The biggest step in any project is the very first step. This book will give you the motivation and knowledge to take not only the first step, but all the other steps to complete the project.

Let's start on the right foot by determining your needs, understanding the various home decorating styles, and learning basic sewing techniques. Decorating your home should be a fulfilling and rewarding experience.

Remember, your home is where you decide to meet challenges, accept opportunities, fight your battles (large or small), fulfill your promises, dare to take on adventures, and yes, share your love. Truly, your home is where your heart is.

Sally Cowan

CHAPTER ONE

Early Decorating Challenges

THEN & NOW

We've come a long way in the home decorating arena since the days of castles and moats. Imagine decorating those damp drafty stone walls! They must have been a home decorator's worst nightmare. The "style" could only be called "purely functional." One thing that hasn't changed through the years is the thrill of going home - to *your* home - and closing the door behind you. "There's no place like home" is as true today as it was in the Garden of Eden.

The room in the Fort Castillo de San Marcos (lovingly called the Old Fort) shows the stark reality of where soldiers once stayed. Only the benches give it a feeling of home. When the Fort was in use a room would include a table, bench, barrels of gun powder and even cannon balls. The Fort was completed in 1695 and is the oldest masonry fort in the continental United States. It was built by the Spanish and the walls are 20 feet thick and 30 feet high. Some of us may think our decorating style is minimalist, but certainly the best example of minimalism is the Old Fort. To appreciate what we have, sometimes we must look at what was.

The rooms in The Oldest House demonstrate minimal home decorating but are certainly an improvement over the Old Fort. In the early 1700s the rooms on this floor housed artillery men, Thomas Gonzalez, and his family. Thomas Gonzalez joined the Castillo garrison as a gunner. Following Spanish custom, the house was sparsely furnished. Chests served as both seats and storage - a reminder to use what you have. Food was both stored and cooked in clay pots and bowls. Charcoal in a brazier on the floor supplied a little warmth.

The moat at the Fort Castillo de San Marcos, Florida.

Fort Castillo de San Marcos was completed in 1695. These benches were made in 1790. Notice the graffiti on the wall - even in those days.

The family slept on straw mats, which were rolled up out of the way during the day. When the British acquired Florida in 1763, the Spanish were forced to leave and the Gonzalez family migrated to Cuba. But while they resided in The Oldest House, they made it a home - *their* home.

The Oldest House in Florida. The foundation was built in 1650 and the structure itself was built in the early 1700s. It was built as a home for a Spanish soldier who was a gunner at the Castillo de San Marcos. We don't know the original owner but a Spanish soldier with a Native American wife lived there in the beginning. It was rebuilt on the same site after a fire in the 1700s.

The Peavetts added a fireplace and window in the British Room.

The stairway leads to the main addition, the second floor (1763-1784 during the British Period).

The Gonzalez Room, circa 1720.

British Major Joseph Peavett (paymaster for England's East Florida troops) and his wife Mary owned the house around 1760. Since the early 1900s, it has been owned by the St. Augustine Historical Society.

The English brought with them more sophisticated furnishings and settled in the comparatively rough surroundings of St. Augustine. Even in these rustic settings, certain pieces of furniture gave the rooms a touch of home, and I'm sure the Peavett family loved entering the place they called home in the year 1763. What caught my attention was the use of personal belongings. A good rule of thumb in home decorating is to work with what you have. The soldiers in the Old Fort and the occupants in The Oldest House did just that.

CHAPTER TWO

Where to Begin - Tools & More

OUR LIVES HAVE BECOME MORE AND MORE MOBILE AND MOST OF US ARE CONSTANTLY IN A STATE OF MOTION. AS A REFLECTION OF THIS, MOST OF OUR HOMES ARE DECORATED WITH SPEED AND CONVENIENCE IN MIND. WE WANT THE STOVE WITHIN REACH OF THE KITCHEN SINK. WE WANT THE BEDROOMS SEPARATE ENOUGH FROM THE REST OF THE HOUSE SO WE DON'T HAVE TO WORRY ABOUT THE BEDS BEING PERFECTLY MADE UP IF UNEXPECTED GUESTS ARRIVE. EVEN THOUGH OUR HOMES ARE UTILITARIAN, SURROUNDING OURSELVES WITH THINGS THAT FEEL FAMILIAR HELPS GIVE THEM A SPECIAL AMBIANCE. WHEN YOU LOOK AT A HOUSE FROM THE OUTSIDE, YOU SEE JUST A HOUSE, BUT WHEN YOU WALK THROUGH THE FRONT DOOR, IT BECOMES A HOME.

TO BEGIN YOUR JOURNEY TOWARD THE SPECIAL HOME YOU DREAMED ABOUT WHEN YOU WERE YOUNG, YOU MUST HAVE A PLAN AND THE RIGHT TOOLS. THE BEAUTY OF DECORATING YOUR OWN HOME IS THAT *YOU* BECOME THE DECORATOR. THIS IS YOUR ADVENTURE. WHAT STARTED OUT AS A SIMPLE OR SMALL HOME DECORATING CHANGE CAN TURN INTO MANY CHANGES THROUGHOUT THE HOUSE.

AS YOU STAND IN THE DOORWAY OF THE ROOM YOU WISH TO DECORATE, NOTICE THE COLORS OF THE RUGS, WALLS, AND WINDOWS. DO YOU WANT THE NEW COLORS TO FLOW FROM ONE ROOM TO THE NEXT, OR WILL THIS ROOM STAND ON ITS OWN? START LOOKING THROUGH MAGAZINES TO SEE WHAT CATCHES YOUR EYE. KEEP A NOTEBOOK OF SWATCHES AND IDEAS AND TAKE IT TO THE FABRIC STORE TO LET YOUR MIND VISUALIZE YOUR IDEAS IN THE FABRICS YOU FIND THERE. ASK FOR HELP AND SUGGESTIONS AND ALLOW YOUR MIND TO BE WIDE OPEN.

JUST LIKE IN ANY PROJECT, THE TOOLS YOU USE FOR HOME DECORATING PROJECTS MAKE A BIG DIFFERENCE. A PLUMBER WOULD NEVER LEAVE HIS TOOLBOX BEHIND. SO LET'S TAKE A LOOK AT THE TOOLS NEEDED IN YOUR VERY OWN "TOOLBOX."

THE
"SEW-A-BEAUTIFUL-HOME" TOOLBOX

Tools left to right: tailor's ham, pin cushion, iron, needles, yardstick, sleeve ham, rotary cutter, scissors, bobbins, covered buttons.

Cutting Tools

Scissors play a large part in the successful outcome of any home decorating project. They must be sharp and comfortable in your hand. For your sewing and home dec projects, keep a high quality pair of scissors separate from your household scissors. If you are left-handed, buy proper left-handed scissors. When purchasing a pair of scissors, make sure they cut through multiple layers of fabric with ease. Since you will be cutting on a flat surface, you might want to consider bent-handled scissors. Check and see if the points of your scissors meet at a precise point. This is the sign of a good pair of scissors.

Tips for Maintaining Cutting Tools

✿ Try not to drop your scissors. Dropping the scissors can affect the alignment.

✿ Oil the screw on your scissors. You should lubricate your scissors every few months. If you cut a lot of adhesives or sticky material, it should be done more often. It is preferable to use a scissors lubricant to oil your scissors. This can be found at some local hardware stores or fabric stores. If this is not available, use a light, low-residue lubricant that wipes dry. Remember to wipe the excess lubricant from your blades before you begin cutting.

✿ Don't open and close your pinking shears without fabric between the blades. The blades are made of similar material and without a buffer, they will grind and wear on each other. Keeping them lubricated will help alleviate this problem. Store your pinking shears closed (this was new information to me).

Bent right-handed or left-handed scissors make it easier to cut on a flat surface.

You can use your whole hand to grip these multi-purpose scissors. I find these wonderful - certainly the best for arthritic hands.

Pinking shears are used to finish off fabric edges that have a tendency to fray. Fiskars Softgrip Pinking Shears are very comfortable to hold.

All-purpose scissors can be used on cardboard, cording, and other light-weight trims.

This small snipping tool is easy to grip.

Use embroidery scissors to trim away detail work.

Rotary cutters are great for cutting strips of fabric through multiple layers.

Pressing Tools

Choosing the right **iron** is very important to the outcome of any sewing project. Keeping the seams pressed as you go will be reflected on the outside of a finished product. Before you rush off to buy whatever iron is on sale, consider the following suggestions.

Choosing the Proper Iron

1. What type of water does the manufacturer recommend? I used distilled water for years until someone told me I should use spring water. What a difference that made. No more rusting.

2. Does the iron have a removable water tank? When using the dry setting on an iron with a removable water tank, it is best to remove the water tank. If it doesn't have a removable water tank, when you are using the dry setting, be sure you empty the water out of the iron. It is best to use spring water rather than distilled water (distilled water can cause rust).

3. Select an iron with a wide range of temperature settings. In most cases the dial will spell this out for you. The first (lowest) setting would be for nylon, second for silk, third for wool, fourth for cotton, and the highest setting for linen.

4. Most new irons have an automatic shut-off to prevent fires. This is a great safety feature, but may be an inconvenience if you repeatedly find the iron has automatically shut off when you return to use it. If you find this annoying, don't buy an iron with an automatic shut-off. But be extra careful to turn it off when you are finished.

5. Make sure the cord can be moved from right to left and left to right.

6. Make sure the sole plate is coated with a nonstick coating. This should be stated on the packaging. Be sure to look for it. If it's not clearly

A steam iron is essential to keep seams pressed flat during construction for a professionally finished look. You'll also need a white, lint-free press cloth.

stated, the iron probably doesn't have a nonstick coating.

7. Choose an iron with a variety of settings for the steam release. Newer irons have a separate dial for steam pressure. It can be set from #1 for a slight steam release to #10 for very forceful steam release. An example of a fabric that needs a higher steam release would be linen.

8. Consider buying a tabletop steam presser. I couldn't live without mine.

Tips for Pressing

❀ Use a white, lint-free press cloth when ironing.

❀ When pressing open a seam, use brown paper between the seam allowance and the fabric. This will eliminate any imprint on the right side of the fabric.

Tailor's Ham - This is a firmly stuffed cushion with rounded curves. Its purpose is for pressing curved areas. Tailor's hams come in different sizes and one side is covered with wool and the other with cotton.

Sleeve Ham - This is also firmly stuffed but is a long tube-like roll with rounded ends. Using a sleeve ham while pressing helps prevent ridges because you to press only the seam, not the surrounding fabric. One side is covered with wool and the other with cotton.

While not essential, a presser is very helpful. Once used only commercially, pressers are now sized for home use.

Tailor's ham.

Sleeve ham.

Sewing Tools

Buy one **pincushion** for the sewing table and another to wear on your wrist. This keeps you from having to constantly look for the pins.

It's best to use **glass or plastic head pins**. For anchoring fabrics to a surface such as a weaving board or ironing board, I recommend long, broad-headed **T-pins**.

For hand sewing, buy a package of **hand sewing needles** in assorted sizes and use the one you're most comfortable with. A **bodkin** is a thick, blunt needle with a long eye. It's ideal to thread cord, ribbon, or elastic through heavy fabrics.

I also recommend a **thimble** to protect your finger. For machine sewing, always begin with a fresh **machine needle** and change it often. Many machine sewing problems are caused by dull needles. Choose the right size and type for the thread and fabric.

A **needle threader** is always handy to have, even if your eyesight is 20/20. You can use it to thread both hand and machine needles.

Upholstery needles are especially handy for pillow tufting or adding a button to a thick pillow.

Choose the proper color, weight, and type of **thread** for the fabric you're sewing on. Best choices are all cotton, cotton wrapped polyester, or all polyester. Don't use those old spools of thread unless you are using them to baste with.

Tacking thread is a special thread type designed specifically for tacking and basting. Because it breaks easily, removing it is much easier than removing conventional sewing thread.

Buy or build a pegboard to keep your thread organized (or sort of organized).

A pegboard is perfect for holding spools of thread.

Needle Size	Weight	Fabric
9	very lightweight	chiffon, sheer
11	lightweight	silk, gingham, cotton
14	medium weight	linen, velvet, chintz, muslin
16	heavyweight	denim, ticking
18	very heavy	canvas, duck

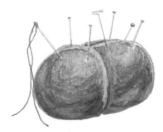

pincushion

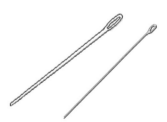

hand sewing needles

needle threader

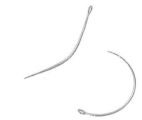

Upholstery needles

CHAPTER THREE

So Many Questions, So Many Colors

BEFORE YOU BEGIN, ASK YOURSELF...

There is always that desire to rush into a project without really thinking it through. The following questions will help you decide what kind of changes make sense for your particular circumstance.

Answering these questions will help direct your planning. For example, if you have others to consider, then you need to talk with them before making major decorating decisions. If your children would prefer to sit in the living room in the evening, then you would want to incorporate a small corner with perhaps a desk for homework. If your life is changing from career to retirement, your choices might lean toward cozy rather than functional. Perhaps the grandkids will be spending more time with you and that extra bedroom will need twin beds instead of a king size bed.

Thinking about windows will help you decide on the appropriate fabric. If you want to let in a lot of light, choose a sheer fabric. If you prefer the room to be dark, choose a heavier fabric.

These questions are just to make you stop and think before you rush into a project and regret some of the decisions later.

1. Where are you at this moment in time in terms of your career and family? Are you ready to retire? Do you have or want a roommate?

2. If there are children at home, do they want a theme room? Incorporate this when changing the room so the child will love spending time in his or her room.

3. Do the children want a special corner in the "adult" room?

4. Do you get bored with the same thing? Do you just want to change small items rather than redo an entire room? Perhaps you just want to add new pillows or a small window treatment.

5. What kind of mood do you want to establish? Do you like a room to be bright and cheery or more subdued? (This helps guide you to choose the correct fabrics.)

6. What style are you trying to achieve? Many styles are described in this book.

7. Who will be using the room?

8. What kinds of fabric do you like? Go to the fabric store and just look at the sea of fabrics.

9. Do you like your windows? What do the windows do for you? Let in air? Light? Serve no purpose at all? Do you like the view? (If not, think about shutters.) How much light do you want to let in? Is your home air-conditioned? Do you prefer open windows?

10. Are there sliding glass doors? Are they used or are they just part of the view? You might decide on vertical blinds, drapes that separate, or no window covering at all.

11. What colors make you feel good? What color in the rainbow is your favorite? Be sure to ask your housemates too.

12. Does your partner have a special chair you need to work into the plan? Don't assume you can just throw it out if it doesn't fit in your new décor.

13. Does your partner have items that must be included, such as a stuffed fish on the wall?

14. Do you like prints or solids? Do you prefer bold prints or paisleys? Go to your fabric store and browse through the fabrics to get a sense of what appeals to you.

15. Do you have pets? Creating a pet area is important to your design.

16. Will you read a lot? In which room? Where in the room? If you love a particular corner for reading, be sure it has lots of light and a comfortable chair.

17. Do you want a television in the room? Will it be part of an "entertainment center" that covers an entire wall?

18. Do you want to recover the furniture or buy new? Consider both and then commit.

19. What is your skill level? Have you ever sewn before? Do you want to take upholstery classes to learn and complete your projects at the same time? Check your area for classes.

20. Most important - check out your clothes closet. What colors dominate your closet? This will tell you a lot about your choices. Read on about how color affects us.

21. The bottom line is this ultimate home decorating question - Do you really want to do this? This seems like a crazy question but a fair one to ask yourself. You "gotta wanna."

THE EFFECTS OF COLOR

Research has proven that colors definitely affect our personality. When you spend time in your home, it's important to feel comfortable. Colors are not only visual but they also create a mood. Studies have shown that light is absorbed into our skin and docs affect how we feel when surrounded by color.

Which color best describes you?

Blue: This is America's favorite color. Blue means trust, loyalty, and honesty. Blue can come across cold but when warm touches are added, it becomes warm and cozy and friendly. It generally has a calming effect but when you use navy, it adds an air of affluence. Blue represents the sky or the deep blue sea and when you add greens or purples, you have a gorgeous combination.

Green: People who love green are caring and giving people. You need to treat these people gently because they have a tendency to get hurt easily. Green reminds us of spring but can also remind us of jealousy. To soften the look, add yellow.

Red: Red doesn't go unnoticed. It creates excitement and evokes feelings of passion. A little bit of this can go a long way. It speeds up our metabolism. If you use pink, it creates a feeling of romance. Reds come in all shades - check out fire engine red or paprika red.

Purple: Purple creates a combination of the excitement of red with the tranquillity of blue. Purple is usually associated with royalty and since we don't see it much in nature, we think of it as an artificial color.

Yellow: Yellow means sunshine and happiness. This is the color of success. If you overuse yellow, you will grow tired of it very quickly.

Orange: Orange doesn't have a great reputation because people think of it as tacky, but subtle shades of orange can create a lovely affect.

Brown: This creates a rustic, natural look. In nature we see rich soil. Browns can be considered a neutral shade or can be combined with rich, muted tones. Try adding touches of green.

White: The color of purity and peace. Overuse of white can cause a room to seem stark and sterile.

Black: Black has long been linked with evil but it also represents elegance and wealth. More and more people are using black in the bathroom.

Where Colors Work Best

- ❧ Blue is ideal for bedrooms or ceilings.
- ❧ Yellow works well in bathrooms and bedrooms.
- ❧ Try green in the living room, but avoid using it in the dining room.
- ❧ Red is very effective in the dining room or library.
- ❧ Neutrals are ideal in the entrance of your home or dining room.

Along with the obvious long-lasting tried-and-true colors, there are a host of hues. Some of the new hues range from khaki, maize yellow, to chameleon shades.

When making home decorating decisions for a child's room, keep in mind that children are color dominant, not shape dominant. Studies indicate that red, blue, and blue-violet are favorite children's colors. Blue is number one on this list. Girls lean towards blue, violet, and green. Boys like blue, red, and green. Keep this in mind when standing in the sea of fabric bolts at the fabric store.

Color matters. Color fills spaces.

CHAPTER FOUR

Glossary – Words You Never Thought You'd Need to Know But . . .

When I first became interested in home decorating, I soon discovered that it had its own language. Because I have sewn for over 30 years, many of the terms were familiar to me, but some were not. Perhaps you are experiencing the same problem. A clear understanding of these words will make home decorating decisions easier. When you go to the fabric store, you will be able to ask questions clearly and concisely by using the proper terms.

In most books, the glossary is found at the end but I feel these words should be up front to clarify terms that are needed now, not when you've reached the end of the book (or your rope).

Appliqué: A decoration applied to a piece of cloth. It can be fused or sewn on.

Balloon shade: A window treatment of shirred or gathered fabric drawn up into billowy folds.

Basting/tacking: These words are interchangeable. Basting means to sew with long, loose stitches to keep the parts together until properly sewn. Tacking means to attach temporarily by sewing with long stitches.

Bed skirt: A long strip of fabric that goes around the box springs and reaches to 1/2″ off the floor. Also called bed ruffle/dust ruffle.

Bias: 45° diagonal to the direction of the weave in fabric.

Bodkin: A thick, blunt needle. A pointed instrument for making holes in cloth.

Bolster: A cylindrical cushion.

Box pleat: A pleat formed by two folded edges - one edge facing right and the other facing left.

Buckram: A coarse cotton, hemp, or linen cloth stiffened with glue or a glue-like substance. This gives a lasting shape to cornices. Also called crinoline.

Bullion fringe: A long, dense fringe. When made from silk or rayon, it adds formality to the room.

Café curtain: Short curtain hung on a rod.

Cascade: Rippling or showering fall of fabric seen in draperies. Also called jabot or tail.

Casing: A fabric pocket to encase a curtain rod or elastic for gathering. Usually made by folding fabric over twice and stitching. Basically a hem with open ends.

Concave: Hollow and curved like a section of the inside of a sphere. An inside curve (think of it like a cave).

Convex: Having a surface that curves outward. An outside curve.

Cornice: An ornamental band for covering a curtain rod. It is made of a rigid panel covered with fabric.

Curtain: Window covering made of fabric, sometimes arranged so that it can be drawn up or sideways. Also to cover, conceal, or shut off something.

Curtain drop: The length of a curtain from the hanging system to the bottom edge.

Cushion: Pillow.

Cut length: The length plus allowances for hems and seams or headers.

Cut width: The width plus allowances for side hems.

Deck: The fabric section of a bed skirt that fits between the mattress and box spring. The decorative skirt is sewn to the deck.

Diameter: The distance across a circle.

Double hem: A hem in which the fabric is turned over twice, usually by the same amount, so the raw edge is completely enclosed.

Drape: The way fabric is hung for a window.

Drapery: A cloth, fabric, textile. Hangings arranged in loose folds. A window treatment that is draped.

Drapery return: The corner at the end of a curtain rod where the rod makes the turn and attaches to the wall.

Drop length: The distance from the top of the object to where you want the fabric to end.

Eclectic: A blending of styles.

Fabric panel: The result of all fabric widths being sewn together.

Finial: Ornamental projection on the end of a curtain pole.

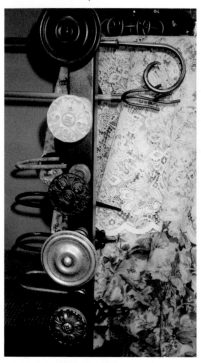

Finished length: The length of the curtain after all hems and headers are sewn.

Finished width: The width of the fabric after all seams and side hems are sewn.

Flange: A projecting rim often seen on pillows.

Frog: Trim made of wrapped cord and formed into loops. Used as a closure.

Fullness: The amount of fabric used over the actual width of an area. Usually 2x, 2½x or 3x or more.

Galloon: Used to cover tacks or nails. Also known as flat braid.

Gather: Bring fabric into a tighter position.

Grain: Either crosswise grain or lengthwise grain. Direction of threads on fabric.

Grainline: This runs parallel to the fabric selvage.

Grommet: A large metal eyelet.

Header: The extra fabric above the curtain rod pocket. Usually for decorative purposes.

Heading tape: Also called pleater tape. A ready-made strip sewn to the top of a curtain and attached to the hanging system. Heading tape is available in various styles. Check your local fabric store for all the types. (See Chapter Twelve for more information.)

Hem: Turning under and stitching a raw edge.

Interfacing: Iron-on or sew-in materials that give bulk and stiffness to areas that need a crisp finish (such as curtain tiebacks).

Interlining: A soft flannel-like fabric, thick cotton, or synthetic material used to line curtains for insulation.

Jabot: see Cascade.

Master slides: The slides that pull the arms that meet in the middle of a curtain rod. This is where there is an overlap when the curtains are pulled shut. Master slides are attached to the draw cord.

Mitering: A way of neatly turning a hem at a corner.

Ottoman: Overstuffed footstool.

Overlap: Where the drapery panels overlap in the center of a two-way traverse rod. The overlap that occurs when the drapes are pulled in a closed position. Also called leading edge.

Pattern repeat: The distance between identical motifs in a pattern.

The total measurement of one complete design. Knowing the distance between the pattern repeats on the fabric is vital in order to join patterned fabric and also is key in determining how much extra fabric to buy.

Pinking: A jagged edge found on pinking shears, used to inhibit raveling on fabric raw edges.

Pinning: To fasten or pierce with a pin. To hold firmly in one place with a pin.

Piping: An edging used on pillows, curtains, valances, and other home decorating areas.

Pleater tape: see Header tape.

Projection: The measurement from the wall to the back of the master slides. Also referred to as the clearance.

Puddle: Drapes that are long enough to lay on the floor. This extra length can be anywhere from 1″ to 18″.

Quilting: The results of sewing a fabric/batting/fabric sandwich together.

Radius: Half of the diameter.

Railroading: When the fabric is turned on its side so the width becomes the length. Used to eliminate seams for sewing valances, cornices, or ruffles.

Return: The measurement from the front of the rod to the wall.

Rod pocket: Flat casing that runs the length of the panel. The curtain rod is inserted in the rod pocket.

Roman shade: Window shade made from fabric that hangs flat when down but folds like an accordion when raised.

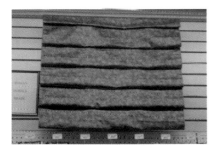

Rope: Thick cord. Plied yarns twisted together.

Rosette: Trim shaped like a rose. Used on pillows and along with swags in window treatments.

Rouleau strip: Narrow tube of fabric strip that can be made into loops. Can be used in place of buttonholes or closures.

Seam: The joint made when two pieces of fabric are sewn together. For an explanation of various seam finishes, refer to Chapter Seven.

Seam allowance: Extra amount of fabric needed to join pieces together. Seam allowances can vary but are usually 1/2″.

Selvage: The lengthwise finished edge that runs down both sides of a length of fabric. Often cut off to avoid puckering.

Swag: Window treatment consisting of cloth loosely draped over a rod. Can be made with or without sewing. Because swags are pulled above the center, they fall in a curve from the center of the cornice board.

Tassel: Hanging ornament that consists of a head and a skirt. Often made out of yarn or ribbon.

Ticking: Tight weave fabric used to enclose a cushion.

Tieback: Device to hold a drapery open. Often a cord, hook, or decorative fabric.

Topstitch: Decorative stitch used to highlight a seamline.

Transitional: Combination of two different styles.

Trapunto: Raised quilted design.

Tuft: Clusters of thread drawn tightly through a pillow, quilt, mattress, to hold the padding in place. Also, a button to which such a tuft is fastened.

Valance: Material used to cover part of a soft furnishing. Often attached to the cornice above curtains or around the base of a bed.

Velcro: Brand name for a nylon strip with hooks and loops. By bringing the opposite sides together, they "hold hands."

Victorian: English decorative style.

Zipper: Metal, plastic, or nylon closure. Can be decorative or heavy duty.

CHAPTER FIVE

Fabrics, Fabrics & More Fabrics

FROM FLAX AND SHEEP'S WOOL TO MANMADE FIBERS, FABRIC IS AS OLD AS MANKIND. FABRIC IS TRULY THE HEART AND SOUL OF HOME DECORATING. AS A SEAMSTRESS, I CAN'T IMAGINE LIFE WITHOUT FABRIC. FABRIC APPEALS TO ALL YOUR SENSES - EMOTIONAL, PHYSICAL, AND SENSUAL.

FABRICS HAVE COME A LONG WAY SINCE THE LOIN CLOTH. EVEN THOUGH FABRICS WERE FIRST WORN FOR PROTECTION AND WARMTH, IT DIDN'T TAKE LONG TO FIND CLOTH COVERING WINDOWS AND USED IN BED COVERINGS. IT IS AT THIS POINT THAT HOME DECORATING GOT ITS START.

TODAY THERE ARE MORE FABRICS THAN EVER TO CHOOSE FROM. IN FACT, WHEN YOU WALK INTO A FABRIC STORE YOU MAY FEEL OVERWHELMED WITH THE CHOICES. MOST FABRIC STORES ARRANGE HOME DECORATING FABRICS ACCORDING TO COLOR AND PATTERN, NOT FABRIC CONTENT. WHEN MAKING A SELECTION, YOU NEED TO TAKE INTO CONSIDERATION HOW THE FABRIC WILL BE USED. THE CHOICE YOU MAKE CAN DETERMINE YOUR STYLE - LACES AND PASTELS FOR ROMANTICS, COTTONS AND FRINGE FOR COUNTRY, LEATHER AND BOLD COLORS COUPLED WITH NEUTRAL TONES FOR CONTEMPORARY, RICH TEXTURES AND BRIGHT STRIPES FOR SOUTHWEST, AND STRONG COLOR SCHEMES FOR ECLECTIC.

Be sure to use "decorator" fabrics because they have a natural drape and are more durable. Remember that finishes are often added to these fabrics to make them resist mildew, stains, and wrinkles, and to have more luster. In garment sewing, we are told to always wash the fabric before making the garment, but with decorator fabrics it is best not to risk washing off the finish.

When planning a decorating project, a good rule of thumb is that the main fabric should equal two thirds of the fabric in the room. That leaves one third that can be broken down into two or three more pieces. For your secondary fabric use accent pieces of prints, plaids, and florals. The prints don't all have to be the same size - go ahead and vary the scale. Plaids work well to accomplish a tailored look. Plaids and prints can be combined using the dominant color in the plaid to pick up a color in the print. Use fabric swatches to mix them up and experiment. Treat them like a puzzle - a puzzle takes time, but the results are worth it.

Fabric Weights

Fabrics come in a variety of weights - sheer, lightweight, medium weight, and heavyweight. This is determined by the number of yarns per inch, fiber types, and size of yarns. This directly affects the drape and feel of the fabric. The following information will help you decide what weight fabric is the most appropriate for your project.

Most upholstery fabrics would be considered heavyweight because they have a backing. The decorator prints are considered medium to lightweight, but the bolts of fabrics don't usually have this marked on them.

Sheer Fabric:

If you can see through a fabric, it can be classified as a sheer. Use sheers if you want to let light in or if you want the surface below it to show through. Sheers are also a good choice if you want lots of gathers for extra fullness.

Lightweight Fabric:

Lightweights are more opaque than sheers, but are still thin and light. Think seersucker or silks. Use lightweights if you want to let a little less light in or if you need lots of gathers. Lightweights are often used as linings for window coverings, but provide minimal privacy if used alone at a window.

Medium Weight Fabric:

Most denim, with the exception of the really heavy stuff, is medium weight. Medium weights work well for window dressings, bed coverings, tablecloths, pillows, and cornices.

Medium weight fabrics are ideal for accessories in a child's room because of their strength and washability.

Heavyweight Fabric:

You'll usually find heavyweight fabrics in the upholstery section of the fabric store. When you need durability, especially in upholstery, choose heavyweights.

Tip

Some fabric stores use what is called a "usage code" for selling home decorating fabrics. The bolts are coded. This code has a master list that suggests that a particular bolt would be best when used for curtains, pillows, bed skirts, etc. Ask the store personnel to help you interpret these codes. Not all bolts of fabrics have these, but it's nice to know they exist.

Fabric Types

The weight of the fabric is very important, but so is the *type* of fabric. When you know the qualities of the fabric, it makes it easier to select the right one for your home decorating project.

Natural Fabrics = Linen, Wool, Cotton, Silk

Linen was the fabric the Egyptians used most often. It is made from the stem of a flax plant. After being spun into yarn, it is woven into fabric. One of the reasons it is perfect for home decorating projects is that it is lint-free and moths don't care for it. The greatest reason to use linen is that it is not damaged by sunlight. Unfortunately, it doesn't hold color well and will look worn in a short time. Linen also wrinkles easily (as you know if you've ever worn a linen dress).

Linen can fray easily, so be sure to finish off the seams (see machine seam finishes in Chapter Seven and serger techniques in Chapter Eight). Linen is also called chambray, damask, and lawn and comes in various textures and finishes. Most linens are blended with synthetic fibers.

Even though **wool** is a natural animal fiber made of protein, it was once considered unclean and was never worn in churches or used in

burials. Wool played an important part in the European textile trade. Wool absorbs moisture and is water-repellent. It resists fading and can be dry cleaned. It does discolor from sunlight, so don't use it to make an item that will be in the direct sunlight. Wool is rather heavy for drapes but it makes a great casual look on upholstery. Wool picks up static electricity and tends to pill. Wool is also called worsted, suit-weight, coat-weight, flannel, tweed, gabardine, challis, and boucle.

Cotton is made from the fibers of a cotton plant. The range of cotton fabrics includes chintz, batiste, broadcloth, denim, gingham, muslin, polished cotton, velour, and sailcloth.

polished cotton

Cotton is used in so many home decorating projects because it is durable, conducts heat well, and drapes well. Like most fabrics, it can weaken if in the sunlight too long. A majority of the fabrics seen in the home decorating department are cottons, cotton blends, or cotton polyesters. Cotton is also referred to as madras, muslin, velvet, drill, cheesecloth, gauze, batiste, chintz, denim, canvas, seersucker, calico, and ticking.

Silk is the only natural filament fiber produced by silkworms. Silk is so versatile because it drapes well and can be combined to make fabrics

that are very sheer to very heavy. Examples of silk are chiffon, brocade, organza, satin, linen, and voile. Silk is great to use for tassels and decorative pillows. Silk is also referred to as georgette, tussah, broadcloth, and taffeta.

Manmade Fabrics = Rayon, Polyester, Nylon, Acrylic, Acetate, Pile, Metallic

Most synthetic fabrics are blends, which makes it possible to combine the good qualities of the blended fabrics and eliminate the bad qualities. If a fabric is 100% synthetic, it will fray easily and you will need to consider seam finishes as detailed in Chapter Seven.

Synthetics are also called Lycra, moiré taffeta, woven velvet, and woven polyester. Synthetic blends are also referred to as cotton/polyester sheeting and permanent press cotton/polyester. Synthetic sheers are also called polyester organza and viscose.

Tip
Cutting silk can be a challenge. To make it easier, pin the fabric to tissue paper before cutting. By cutting the paper and the silk at the same time, the fabric won't shift. This is a tip experts use all the time.

Rayon is made from wood and other cellulose products. It was introduced in 1889 and quickly became popular because of its silky quality.

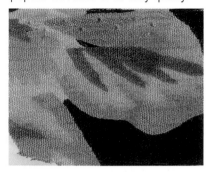

Rayon is soft and drapes well. It fades if left in the sunlight over a long period of time. Use rayon for bedspreads, tablecloths, and draperies (you'll probably want to line the draperies for privacy and to protect the fabric from the sun).

Polyester blends are easy to dye and are colorfast. Polyester resists moths and mildew and, when used in

curtains, retains heat-set-in pleats. It is also wrinkle proof and resists sun rot.

Nylon will fade and in time will rot in the sun. On the other hand, it is durable and has insulating qualities, which make it a good choice for out-

erwear. For home dec projects it is not suitable for unlined draperies, drapery linings, or any outdoor furnishings.

Acrylic is wrinkle proof and also has insulating qualities. Over time, the color will darken in the sun. Use acrylic as an interlining.

Acetate will wrinkle but does resist mildew and sun rot. Acetate is a good choice for a lining fabric.

Pile fabrics are challenging and have to be cut in the same direction to avoid a difference in color. Because of this, you need more fabric for the project. The nap can go either up or down, but be consistent

in all the pieces. Popular uses for pile fabrics are stuffed animals, decorative pillows, or fun accent pieces. Pile fabrics are also called faux or fake fur, velvet, velveteen, corduroy, and terrycloth.

Metallics are used traditionally for evening wear but could be used for small accent pieces such as a small designer pillow. Woven metallics include sequined fabric and gold lamé, with or without backing. Knitted metallics include satin, knitted sheer, sequined knit, and smooth metallic knit.

Use **waterproof fabric** for shower curtains, outdoor tablecloths, lawn furniture, and fitted sheets for a baby's bed.

Fabrics Not Seen = Interfacing, Interlining

Interfacing is also called fusible, iron-on, and tailor's linen. There are well over 100 different interfacings. Interfacing is just an additional layer of fabric that goes between the outer layer and the facing/lining or hem. Interfacing is added to give additional strength and prevent sagging.

Interlining is a flannel-like fabric used to give fabrics a more luxurious feel and to insulate. You can enhance the look of lesser quality fabric by using interlining. This is in addition to lining. Interlining is also called bump.

FABRICS AT A GLANCE

Here is a list of the most commonly used fabric terms and a short definition for each.

Acetate: synthetic fiber made from cellulose acetate. Because it is soft and pliable, it resembles silk.

Acrylic: combination of cellulose and acetate that forms flakes. When the flakes are dried, they are dissolved in acetone and are extruded through spinnerets.

Border print: design usually along the selvage edge of fabric. It can be printed, woven, or embroidered.

Broadcloth: rayon or cotton with a small ribbed pattern in the weave.

Brocade: design woven in cotton, silk, wool, or synthetic fiber combinations. There is a raised design on a flat surface.

Buckram: thick and stiffened jute linen or cotton. Gives shape to cornices.

Burlap: coarse woven cloth often used for upholstery fabric.

Calico: plain-weave cotton fabric with small motifs.

Canvas: multiple-ply yarn that is stiff and plain-woven. Example is sailcloth.

Challis: rayon, cotton, wool, or synthetic fabric. Sold in solid colors, vivid floral prints, and paisley patterns.

Chintz: because of a glaze finish, chintz has a surface shine. This is a tightly woven cotton fabric and comes in various colors and prints.

Corduroy: pile or napped fabric with ridges or cords. Made from cotton or rayon.

Cotton: absorbent fiber made from the cotton plant. The basis for many fiber combinations.

Damask: the various fibers of damask give it a flat and reversible woven jacquard design. The combined plain and satin weaves make it great for many home decorating ideas. Damask is usually one color.

Decorator fabric: fabric that is durable because of three factors - fiber content, number of yarns used in the manufacturing process, and the finishing process.

Denim: heavy cotton cloth (one we all love).

Duck: closely woven cotton fabric similar to canvas.

Gabardine: made from cotton, wool, rayon, or nylon with a twill weave.

Gingham: along with the usual checked print, this fabric can also be plaid, striped, or solid. It is a yarn-dyed, plain weave cotton or synthetic fabric.

Jacquard: reversible tapestry.

Linen: fabric made from a flax plant. Can be of various weights.

Lining: usually silk, cotton, or a blend; used to protect seams.

Moiré: plain, ribbed weave of silk, cotton, or rayon. You will see a watermark pattern on this fabric.

Muslin: a soft woven cotton. You will find muslin bleached or unbleached, light or heavy.

Nap: fuzzy fibers on the surface of some fabrics such as corduroy, or velour.

Nylon: the very first synthetic fiber. Usually wrinkle-resistant and easy to wash.

Percale: like muslin, but with a finer texture.

Pile: Uncut loops on the surface of fabric such as terrycloth.

Polished cotton: plain-weave cotton with a permanent glaze finish.

Polyester: synthetic fiber with a tendency to not "breath" so can be very hot to wear.

Poplin: lightweight fabric with the same size warp and filling yarns as cotton.

Pre-quilted: fabric that has already been machine quilted to a layer of padding.

Rayon: man-made fiber made from recycled cellulose.

Sateen: imitation satin.

Satin: weave fabric with a glossy finish on the front and dull finish on the back.

Seersucker: fabric that gets its appearance from alternating puckered stripes with flat ones.

Silk: fiber made by silkworms.

Tapestry: heavy fabric with a woven pattern in it.

Terrycloth: features uncut loops on one or both sides of the cloth.

Ticking: closely woven satin or twill weave, usually in linen or cotton. Striped ticking is the most popular, with a narrow colored strip on a white or cream background.

Velour: fabric with a thick, short, warp pile. Not too absorbent. It is usually made of a man-made fiber or blend.

Velvet: a nap or pile fabric, with short pile on the front on a woven background.

Velveteen: unlike velvet, this has an extra set of filling yarns. On a woven background.

Vinyl: fabric with a vinyl base.

Voile: made from a tightly twisted yarn; has a semi-sheer feel.

Wool: natural animal fiber made of protein.

RIGHT FABRIC + RIGHT PROJECT = SUCCESS!

The fabric you choose dictates the style you achieve. For example:

❧ For the Victorian look, use brocades in rich colors, tapestries, and velvets. Suggested accessories are sumptuous window treatments with trims and tassels, antiques or reproduction period pieces, and gilded mirrors.

❧ For the American country look use fabrics in natural fibers, muslin, plaids, and checks. Keep to simple lines - pine pieces and an overall homespun look.

❧ For the English country look, choose floral chintzes and coordinates in beautiful colors.

Suggested accessories are needlepoint pillows, cozy furnishings, ruffles, fresh flowers, and a tea set.

❧ For the contemporary look, use natural fabrics in neutral tones and monochromatic schemes - leathers or animal prints. Use straight clean lines. Suggested accessories are burnished metals and varying geometric shapes.

❧ For the southwestern look, choose woven fabrics, leather, desert pastels, or bold designs. Suggested accessories are cacti, animals, and Native American blankets and artwork.

❧ For the traditional look, use moiré, velvet, brocade, or silk.

❧ For the eclectic look, use four to six different fabrics. Basically a combination of various styles.

❧ In informal settings, use chintz, linen, seersucker, and cotton sateen. Also calico, canvas, corduroy, denim, gabardine, ticking, poplin, gingham, or burlap.

From the fig leaf to fabrics printed with leaves, the choice is endless.

Fabrics fill spaces.

Item	Suggested Fabric
Pillows	polished cotton, textured cotton, velveteen, corduroy, linen, chintz
Draperies	jacquard, denim, chintz
Café curtains	gingham, calico
Kitchen curtains	cotton, cotton blend, chintz
Child's room curtains	polished cotton, decorator fabric, denim
Office curtains	lightweight blend fabric, linen, denim
Bedspread	broadcloth, pre-quilted fabric, gingham
Bed ruffle	cotton blend, cotton, polished cotton
Pillow sham	closely woven fabric, washable fabric
Pillowcase	muslin, cotton
Shower curtain	broadcloth, chintz, calico, gingham
Tablecloth	brocade, cotton blend, border print
Napkins	cotton, cotton blend
Appliance cover	broadcloth, terrycloth
Stool cover	broadcloth, canvas, sateen, tapestry
Chair cover	broadcloth, calico, damask, moiré
Valance	polished cotton, cotton blend
Cornice	buckram, padded fabrics, decorator fabrics
Computer cover	duck, cotton blend
Boat interior	duck

CHAPTER SIX

Measure Up –
Measure Twice, Cut Once

TO HELP YOU APPROXIMATE THE AMOUNT OF FABRIC NECESSARY TO MAKE A PROJECT, I'VE INCLUDED THE BASIC MEASUREMENTS OF A MATTRESS, BED PILLOW, BEDSPREAD, DUST RUFFLE, COMFORTER, TABLECLOTH, NAPKINS, AND READY-MADE DRAPERIES. THIS GIVES YOU A QUICK IDEA OF THE BASIC SIZES. THAT DOESN'T MEAN YOU WILL STICK TO THESE MEASUREMENTS, BUT THEY WILL HELP YOU JUDGE HOW MUCH FABRIC YOU MIGHT NEED AND THEREFORE HOW MUCH THE PROJECT MIGHT COST. KEEP THIS HANDY AS A QUICK REFERENCE.

BASIC MEASUREMENTS

A queen size bed is perfect for a teenager. This one is covered with a wedding ring quilt. Something old, something new.

Mattress:

Twin 39″ x 75″
Full 54″ x 75″
Queen 60″ x 80″
King 76″ x 80″
California King 72″ x 84″

A day bed can be used as a sofa or a guest bed.

Day Bed Mattress:

39″ x 75″
Note: Day beds vary in size.

Great things come in small packages. This crib is complete with a canopy and bed ruffle.

Crib Mattress:

27″ x 54″

Adjust the size to fit the doll. This size is perfect for popular 18-inch dolls such as American Girls™ or Creative Doll®.

Doll Bed Mattress:

12″ x 26″

Pillows are terrific accents and there are so many choices - flange, square, piped, fringed, ruffled, or plain.

Bed Pillow:

Standard 20″ x 26″
Queen 20″ x 30″
King 20″ x 36″

How did we ever survive without king size beds? This one features a damask cover and a tailored bed skirt.

Comforter/Bed Cover:

Twin 69″ x 90″
Full 84″ x 90″
Queen 90″ x 95″
King 104″ x 92″
California King 110″ x 96″

This quilted bedspread and coordinating upholstered headboard personalize a summer home.

Bedspread:

(standard drop of 21″ but can vary)

Twin 81″ x 110″
Full 96″ x 110″
Queen 102″ x 115″
King 120″ x 115″
California King 120″ x 115″

Bed Skirt Deck:
(the fabric that goes under the

mattress to hold the bed skirt)

Twin 39″ x 75″
Full 54″ x 75″
Queen 60″ x 80″
King 76″ x 80″
California King 72″ x 84″

Waterbed Mattress:

Super Single 48″ x 84″
Queen 60″ x 84″
King 72″ x 84″
Note: Now you know why your fitted sheets won't fit your waterbed.

Inflatable Mattress:

Twin 39″ x 74″
Full 54″ x 74″
Queen 60″ x 78″

You can combine colors and styles by using more than one layer in your table covering.

A bright and cheerful kitchen area with brick red and yellow napkins and place mats to coordinate with the chairs.

Tablecloth:

(standard drops vary - for a dining table, it's usually 10″-12″, for a formal dining room, it's usually 16″-24″, and many are floor length)

52″ x 52″
52″ x 70″
60″ x 84″
60″ x 102″
60″ x 120″
60″ x 144″
70″ round
90″ round

Napkins:

Cocktail 12″ square
Luncheon 14″ square
Dinner 16″ square

I used a cotton fabric printed with stripes and floral designs for these pinch pleated lined curtains. The fluted wooden pole and hand stained wood rings work well with the fabric.

Draperies:

(standard ready-made measurements)

48″ x 63″
48″ x 84″
72″ x 84″
96″ x 84″

Valance:

(to match Draperies as listed above)

48″ x length desired
72″ x length desired
96″ x length desired

This shower curtain features a cotton print with a bordered flounce.

Shower Curtain:

72″ x 72″
*Note: You can adjust the length if you like
a longer shower curtain.*

Bathrooms can be just as elegant as any room. This embroidered sheer shower curtain combines very subtle shades of gray for an understated look.

CALCULATING YARDAGE

Measuring your bed, table, or windows can be done quickly if you follow these simple instructions. People often pay a professional to take measurements and if you feel that would work for you, then that's what you should do. But before you rush to hire an interior decorator, read the following information and see if you feel comfortable doing your own measuring.

MEASURING FOR A
ROUND TABLECLOTH

A "decorator" table covered with a full length round chintz tablecloth edged with a shirred jumbo rope cord.

Table Diameter	Yardage amt. for a 10″ drop		Trim amt. for a 10″ drop	Yardage amt. for a 30″ drop	Trim amt. for a 30″ drop
	45″ or 54″			45″ or 54″	
30″	2⅞ yds.	1½ yds.	4¼ yds.	5½ yds.	8 yds.
36″	3¼ yds.	3¼ yds.	5 yds.	5½ yds.	8½ yds.
48″	4 yds.	4 yds.	6 yds.	6 yds.	9½ yds.
54″	4¼ yds.	same	6½ yds.	9½ yds.	10 yds.
60″	4½ yds.	same	7 yds.	10 yds.	10½ yds.
66″	5 yds.	same	7½ yds.	10½ yds.	11 yds.
72″	7¾ yds.	5¼ yds.	8 yds.	11 yds.	11½ yds.

Yardage and Trim Chart for a Round Tablecloth

Note: The trim amount is the yardage needed for the trim to go around the outside edge of a tablecloth with a 10″ drop, 30″ drop, etc.

D diameter (the longest distance from one side to the other)
DR drop (the distance from the tabletop to where you want the length to end)

For the cutting width, add twice the drop to the table diameter plus 1″. Piece several widths of fabric together if necessary. The cutting length is identical to the width.

Measure the diameter of the table	= _____ ″ **D**
Measure the drop	= _____ ″ **DR**
Diameter	_____ ″ **D**
Add two times the drop (**DR** x 2)	+ _____ ″
Add 1″ for the hem	+ 1″
Total this	= _____ ″ (cutting width of fabric)

* If the cutting width is greater than the width of your fabric, you will need to purchase two lengths of fabric.

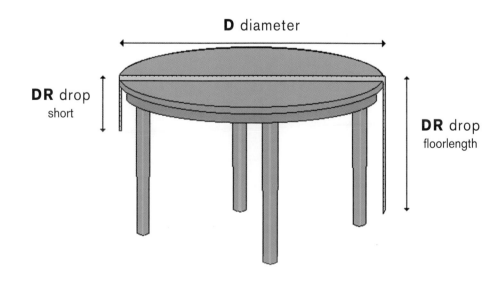

D diameter

DR drop
short

DR drop
floorlength

MEASURING FOR A SQUARE/RECTANGULAR TABLECLOTH

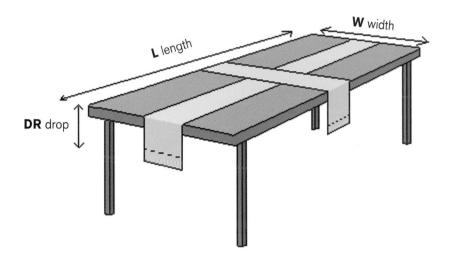

For the cutting width, multiply the drop by 2, then add the table width plus 1″. For the cutting length, multiply the drop by 2, then add the table length plus 1″.

Measure the width of the tabletop	=	_____″ **W**
Measure the drop	=	_____″ **DR**
Width		_____″ **W**
Add two times the drop (**DR** x 2)	+	_____″
Add 1″ for the hem	+	1″
Total this	=	_____″ (cutting width of fabric)
Measure the length of the tabletop	=	_____″ **L**
Add two times the drop (**DR** x 2)	+	_____″
Add 1″ for the hem	+	1″
Total this	=	_____″ (cutting length of fabric)

MEASURING FOR BEDDING ITEMS

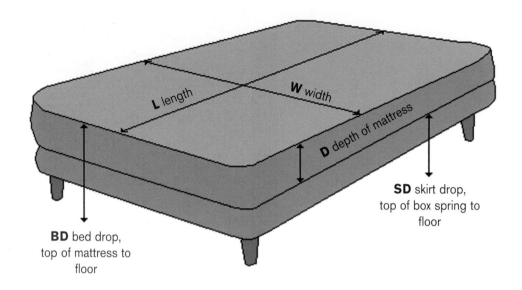

L length **W** width **D** depth of mattress

SD skirt drop, top of box spring to floor

BD bed drop, top of mattress to floor

Before measuring, be sure your bed is made up with all extras such as sheets, blankets, and comforters. This is especially necessary when measuring the drop. It will make a difference.

Bedspread

For the cutting width, add twice the bed drop measurement to the mattress width plus 4″. For the cutting length, add the bed drop measurement minus 1/2″ plus 16″ to the mattress length.

Measure the width of the mattress	=	_____ ″ **W**
Measure the bed drop	=	_____ ″ **BD**
Width		_____ ″ **W**
Add two times the drop (**BD** x 2)	+	_____ ″
Add 4″ for the hem	+	4″
Total this	=	_____ ″ (cutting width of fabric)
Measure the length of the mattress	=	_____ ″ **L**
Add the drop minus 1/2″ (**BD** - 1/2″)	+	_____ ″
Add 14″ for pillow tuck-in	+	14″
Add 2″ for the hem	+	2″
Total this	=	_____ ″ (cutting length of fabric)

If you are using repeat patterned fabric:
Multiply the cutting length by the repeat inches = _____ ″

Bed Skirt

Move the mattress off your bed to take accurate measurements of the box spring. Measure the width from edge to edge and measure the length from top to bottom. For the length of the ruffle, measure from the top of the box spring to 1/2″ off the floor.

A cotton floral bed ruffle trimmed in contrasting fabric.

Bed Skirt Deck

For the cutting width, add 1″ to the width of the box spring. For the cutting length, add 2½″ to the length of the box spring.

Measure the width of the box spring	=	_____″ **W**
Add 1″		+ 1″
Total this	=	_____ (cutting width of deck fabric)
Measure the length of the box spring	=	_____″ **L**
Add 2½″	+	2½″
Total this	=	_____″ (cutting length of deck fabric)

> ### Tip
> Instead of buying fabric and making a deck for your bed skirt, use an old fitted bed sheet.

Gathered Bed Skirt

For the cutting length of the skirt, multiply the three-sided perimeter measurement by 2½. For the cutting width of the skirt, add 6″ to the skirt drop (from the box spring to 1/2″ off the floor). Piece widths together if necessary to achieve the necessary width. The finished skirt will hang 1/2″ off the floor.

Measure the length of the bed	=	_____″ **L**
Measure the width of the bed	=	_____″ **W**
Double the length (**L** x 2)	=	_____″
Add the width (**W**)	+	_____″
Total this	=	_____″
Multiply the total by 2½ for fullness	=	_____″ (cutting length of skirt)
Measure the drop from the box spring to the floor	=	_____″ **SD**
Add 6″ for hem, seam allowance	+	6″
Total this	=	_____″ (cutting width of skirt)

Tailored Bed Skirt

First calculate the drop (length of skirt)

Measure from the top of the mattress to 1/2″ from floor		_____	**D**
Add 2″ (hem allowance) and 1/2″ (seam allowance)	+	2½″	
Total drop	=	_____	**TD**

Next calculate the width (around the bed)

Total width of bed		_____	**W**
Add the length of bed x 2 (**L** x 2)	+	_____	
Total this	=	_____	**T**
T x 2½″	=	_____	**SW** (skirt width)

For two 12″ pleats, one at each foot corner, add 24″ to the skirt width (**SW**). Divide this figure by 54″ to arrive at the number of cut lengths. Multiply the number of cut lengths by the total drop (**TD**) and divide by 36″ to arrive at the total yardage required.

Bed Cap

Measure the length of the mattress	=	_____ ″	**L**
Measure the width of the mattress	=	_____ ″	**W**
Measure the depth of the mattress	=	_____ ″	**D**
Double the mattress depth (2 x **D**)	=	_____ ″	
Add the length of the mattress	+	_____ ″	**L**
Add 5″ for hems	+	5″	
Total this	=	_____	(cutting length of fabric)
Double the mattress depth (2 x **D**)	=	_____ ″	
Add the width of the mattress	+	_____ ″	
Add 3″ for hems	+	3″	
Total this	=	_____	(cutting width of fabric)

Here's a quick reference guide for the amount of yardage required for various bedding items. If you are using a print, allow an extra yard of fabric.

Bedspread			
	36″	48″	54″
Twin	12 yds.	8 yds.	8 yds.
Full	12 yds.	12 yds.	8 yds.
Queen	15 yds.	12 yds.	12 yds.
King	15 yds.	12 yds.	12 yds.

Comforter (54″ wide)	
Twin, Full, Queen	7 yds.
King	11 yds.

Pillow Sham (54″ wide)	
Simple sham	1½ yds.
Sham with ruffles	3 yds.

Bed Skirt (54″ wide)							
Gathered Skirt				Tailored skirt			
Twin	Full	Queen	King	Twin	Full	Queen	King
7½ yds.	8¼ yds.	8¼ yds.	9 yds.	6 yds.	6 yds.	6 yds.	6¾ yds.

MEASURING FOR A VALANCE

A valance is a quick and easy way to add an accent to a window. Great fabric choices are cotton prints, stripes, cotton blends, and solid cottons. A simple gathered valance is an easy beginner project.

Before measuring for your valance, have the hardware already installed. It's important to decide where you plan to hang the valance before beginning. You can hang it on the window frame, inside the window frame, beyond the window frame, or above the window frame. Where you hang will affect your measurements.

The average valance is 10″ to 16″ from top to bottom. This includes a 2″ header (a fabric extension above the rod). When measuring for the valance height, always measure from the top of the rod to where you want the valance to end. Add a hem allowance and extra for a header if you plan to have one.

Some valances include cascades. When deciding on the length of the cascades, be sure you get the correct proportions. Keep this home decorating rule of thumb in mind: think in thirds. The valance's center drop should extend one third of the way down the top half of the window. The tails or cascades should extend one to two thirds of the way down the whole window.

A single valance with a 3″ header made from multi-colored chintz.

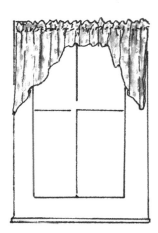 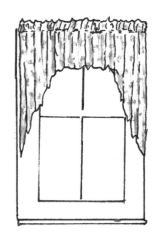 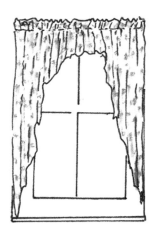

With all valances, always allow enough fabric for fullness at the window. A good rule to follow is to multiply the width of the curtain rod by three. This gives a professional look, which is the goal you want to achieve. (Refer to Chapter Twelve for instructions for making valances.)

As an example, here is the formula for figuring the amount of fabric needed for a *one-rod pocket, self-lined* valance with a *3″ header*.

Measure the height of the valance	= ____″ **A**	
Double this for self-lining (**A** x 2)	= ____″	
Add 13″ for hems and headings	+ 13″	
Total this	= ____″ (cutting length of fabric)	
Measure the width of the rod	= ____″ **B**	
Triple this for fullness (**B** x 3)	= ____″ (cutting width of fabric)	

MEASURING WINDOWS FOR CURTAINS/DRAPERIES

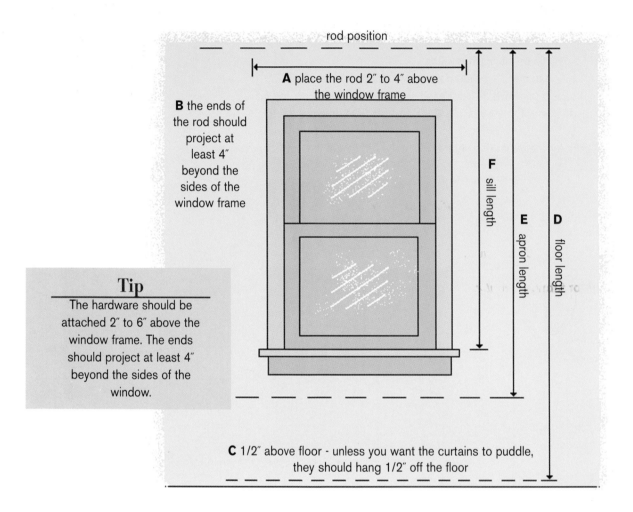

rod position

A place the rod 2″ to 4″ above the window frame

B the ends of the rod should project at least 4″ beyond the sides of the window frame

F sill length

E apron length

D floor length

Tip
The hardware should be attached 2″ to 6″ above the window frame. The ends should project at least 4″ beyond the sides of the window.

C 1/2″ above floor - unless you want the curtains to puddle, they should hang 1/2″ off the floor

For accurate measurements, mount your hardware first. Use a metal tape measure and measure each window separately. Even though windows may look exactly alike, they could vary enough to make a difference. Don't take the chance. (Refer to Chapter Twelve for instructions for making curtains and drapes.)

When Calculating the Finished Length

❀ If your fabric has a pattern repeat, measure the distance between motifs and add one repeat per cutting length.

❀ If you want a casing but no heading, add 1/2″ to the diameter of the rod for turning under and another 1/4″ to 1″ (depending on the thickness of the fabric) for ease in handling.

❀ For the bottom hems, add double the desired hem to the finished length.

❀ If using sheer or lightweight fabric, allow for a 5″ to 6″ double hem by adding 10″ to 12″ to the length.

❀ If using medium weight fabric for floor length curtains, allow for a 4″ double hem by adding 8″ to the length

❀ If making short curtains or a valance, allow for a 1″ to 3″ double hem by adding 2″ to 6″ to the length.

Calculate the Finished Length

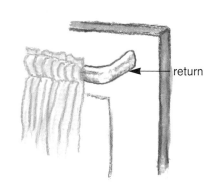

return

❧ Measure from the top of the rod or heading to the desired length (sill, apron, or floor).
❧ Add hem allowances, casing measurements, heading, and pattern repeats if applicable. This is the finished cutting length.

When Calculating the Finished Width

❧ Adjust for the desired fullness. This will depend on the weight of the fabric. For medium to heavyweight fabrics, add 2 to 2½ times the finished width. For sheer and lightweight fabrics, add 2½ to 3 times the finished width.
❧ If the panels are not wider than the fabric, you don't need to add any extra for seam allowances. If there are multi-panels, add 1″ for each seam.
❧ Add 4″ per panel for side hems. This results in a 1″ double-fold hem on each side of the panel.
❧ Don't forget to add extra for the return (the short ends of the rod that stand out from the wall).

Calculate the Finished Width

* Measure the rod width and add the return.

To figure yardage for fabric *without a pattern match*:

Finished length	=	_____″
Add bottom hem doubled	+	_____″
Add casing & headings	+	_____″
Total this	=	_____″ (cutting length of fabric)

Finished width	=	_____″
Multiply the width by fullness factor (2½ or 3)	=	_____″
Add side hems and seams as applicable	+	_____″
Total this	=	_____″ (cutting width of fabric)

To figure yardage for fabric *with a pattern repeat:* (the length doesn't change)

Distance between pattern repeats	=	_____″
Multiply by finished width	=	_____″ (cutting width of fabric)

Whether you are taking measurements on areas in your home or on your body, it isn't going to be your favorite part of the project. It can be quite challenging at times but it's a necessary step. With this behind you, let's move on to the goal.

Inches fill spaces.

CHAPTER SEVEN

Sewing Machine Techniques

There are certain machine stitches that are used over and over again no matter what the project. It always helps to get to know your sewing machine by first reading over the manual, if you can find it. "When all else fails, read the instructions." No matter what the project, it will have corners, curves, and straight lines.

SEWING CURVES

Inside and outside curves are common when sewing home decorations. Outside curves require clipping into the seam allowance. Snip away little triangles of the fabric to reduce the bulk. For the inside curve, just clip into the seam allowance.

Snip triangles on outside curves to reduce bulk.

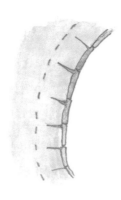

Clip inside curves into the seam allowance.

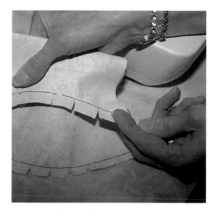

A clipped inside curve is shown above a clipped outside curve.

WHICH MACHINE IS BEST?

When it comes to choosing the proper sewing machine, please ask yourself these questions before you enter the store.

- What will I use the machine for?
- How much money am I willing to spend?
- Do I want to do a lot of embroidery?
- Does the machine thread easily?
- Does the store offer classes?
- Do I trust their repair department?

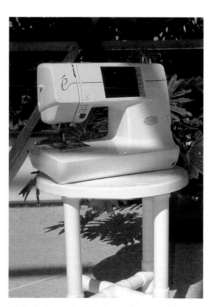

This baby lock ESe2 sewing machine is just one example of how the industry has advanced. This machine features built-in touch screens, a myriad of stitch selections, and unlimited embroidery capabilities.

When you go to the store, sit down and actually sew on the sewing machine. I personally check out the noise level because I like a machine that purrs. If that is important to you, pay close attention when you are running the machine. Don't just sew the basic stitches - try as many utility stitches as possible and experiment with the built-in decorative stitches.

Find out if the store offers classes. Ask about their service policy. Ask for referrals and talk to others who have purchased the machine you are interested in. Check for comparative consumer reports. Weigh the pros and cons of different brands and different models. A sewing machine is an investment. Take as much time as you need to make a decision.

BASIC SEWING MACHINE TECHNIQUES

Continuous Bias Strips - Option #1

I thought I knew the best way to create a continuous bias until I saw this "magic" trick. Once you have done it this way, you will never look back. You will be amazed how much cording you can make from a small scrap of fabric.

1. If you have a piece of fabric long enough, fold it in half and stitch around all three sides. If you don't have a piece that can be folded, stitch two pieces together and sew all four sides. Use a 1/2″ seam allowance. Letter or number the corners.

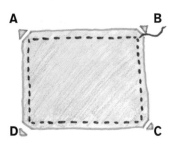

2. Clip across all four corners, past the stitching point (something you would *never* normally do).

3. Using a straight edge, draw a line from the upper left corner to the lower right corner (from **A** to **C**). Cut on this line *on the top layer only*. Flip the fabric over and draw a line from the upper right corner to the lower left corner (from **B** to **D**). Cut on this line, this layer of fabric only.

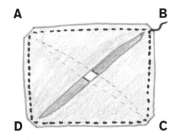

4. Now you have a rectangle with diagonal seams. Carefully press the seams open. This is a bias piece of

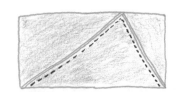

fabric, so try not to distort it by stretching the fabric. Be careful how you handle the fabric at this point.

5. Using a straight edge ruler, draw a line 6″ to 9″ from the left fold line. The wider the cording you are going to make, the wider this will be.

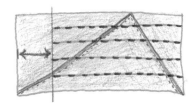

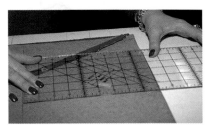

6. Measure the circumference of your cording and add 1″. This number will be the width of the strips. Mark your fabric with horizontal lines using the above measurement only up to the vertical line.

Cut on these lines. Open up your fabric and you will notice that it now looks like a windsock.

7. Open this tube of strips. The 6″ (narrow) to 9″ (wide) cord fold area is opened to twice the width. Lay this all flat on the table.

8. Mark diagonally, starting from the left upper corner to the bottom of the top strip.

9. Cut along the diagonal lines. Believe it or not, you now have one piece of continuous bias stripping, all from a relatively small piece of fabric. Place the cord in the fabric and using the zipper foot, make your corded trim.

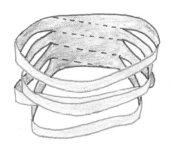

The width of the strip is determined by the size of the cord. The bigger the cord, the wider the strip.

Continuous Bias Strips - Option #2

Here's another way to make a continuous bias strip. Follow the steps below and it should be quick, easy, and painless.

1. Fold down the corner of the fabric so the crosswise edge is aligned with the selvage.

2. Using that fold, measure and mark 1½" wide strips. The larger the cord, the larger the strips. Mark on the wrong side of the fabric.

3. Bring the short ends together with right sides together, with one end extending above the other. It will look like a tube. Stitch the ends together with a 1/4" seam allowance.

4. Cut along the line, making a continuous strip.

5. Join these long continuous strips together if you need more length. Place the cord inside the strips to make the cording/piping.

Tip

If your stitches are skipping, change the machine needle.

SEAM FINISHES

A serger is wonderful for eliminating frayed edges, but not everyone owns a serger. And even if you do, there are some seams that are best done using the sewing machine. All the "tried and true" seam finishes still work. A plain seam is the quickest and easiest way to join two pieces of fabric. Simply pin the fabric right sides together and sew along the seam line, taking out the pins as you sew. Remember to backstitch at the beginning and end of each seam to add strength.

Flat Fell Seam

A flat fell seam is a great seam for strength. This is the seam used on jeans. This seam shows on the right side of the fabric, which you need to consider.

1. Sew the fabric right sides together with a 5/8″ seam allowance.

Right sides together.

2. Trim away one seam allowance to 3/16″.

3. Fold the wide seam over the narrow one and turn the raw edge under. Pin or tack this down.

4. Sew along the folded edge and press. Use your machine foot to guide you.

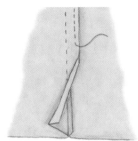

Use your machine foot to guide the stitching.

French Seam

A French seam finish won't show on the right side of the fabric. You can only use this on straight edges and must allow 5/8″ for the seam allowance.

1. Put the fabric *wrong* sides together and sew 3/16″ from the edge.

Wrong sides together.

2. Trim both seam allowances to 1/8″ and press flat.

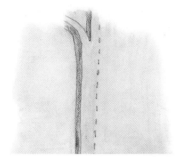

Trim the seam.

3. Turn the fabric so the right sides are together. Sew a second seam 3/8″ from the fold. The raw edges are hidden inside the seam. Press the seam to one side.

The raw edges are hidden inside the seam.

Zigzag Seam

For a zigzag seam, set your machine for the zigzag stitch and sew along the raw edge, keeping the needle close to the edge so it stays on the fabric. This can be done with the seam open or closed.

The zigzag stitch is great for gathering. Use a heavy cord or even elastic, and zigzag over it, being sure not to catch the cord. Catch one end and pull the other. Instant gathers.

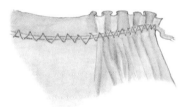

Bias Binding

For bias binding on the seam:

1. Unfold one edge of the bias tape and line it up with the raw edge.

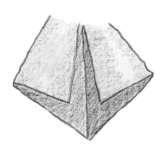

2. Sew the binding on, matching the raw edge with right sides together. Sew slightly left of the bias fold. Trim the edge.

Trim the edge.

3. Fold the binding over the raw edge and sew it down through all the layers from the top side.

4. Stitch in the ditch, using the seamline.

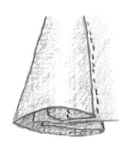

Stitch in the ditch, using the seamline.

Pinking

Pinking is a quick way to neaten a raw edge. Pinking shears cut a serrated edge. This is not a long-lived method so other seam finishes might be a better choice.

1. Put the seam allowances together and trim.

2. Press the seam open.

HEMMING

Once you have your curtain measured and cut accurately, you shouldn't have to worry about the curtain fitting the window after it is hemmed. It is easier to sew the bottom hem first, then the side hems, then the casing, and last the heading.

In unlined curtains, the side hems and bottom hems are doubled to add weight and strength. When measuring for a double fold hem, use a seam gauge as you go to keep the width consistent and pin as you fold.

1. Turn the bottom hem under 3″ and press. Turn under another 3″, pin, and press.

A double fold hem, pinned and ready to sew.

2. For the side seams, turn 1″ to the wrong side. Pin and press. Fold under another 1″. Pin and press. If you are using weights, tack the weights inside the second fold at the seams and side corners.

3. After pressing, stitch using a straight stitch on your sewing machine.

Hem Finishing

There are various ways to finish off the hem.

❧ **Straight stitch**. Sew a straight stitch on the folded hem edge. This is usually a double fold.

❧ **Machine blindhem stitch**. Use the hemming foot for your sewing machine. After you've pressed the fold, turn the hem back to the right side. You will need to leave a fold of fabric 1/8″ from the hem edge. Stitch on this small edge with blindhem stitch.

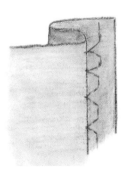

❧ **Fuse the hem**. Place a strip of fusible web between the pressed hem. Use a damp press cloth and hold the heat on the hem for approximately 15 seconds. This isn't my favorite way of doing a hem. Although it is almost permanent, if you wash the curtains I wouldn't want to bet money on this hem staying put.

Corner Mitering - Option #1

1. If you are mitering trim or lace, simply place the two lengths right sides together. Fold the top trim at a right angle to form a diagonal corner. Press and baste this diagonal fold.

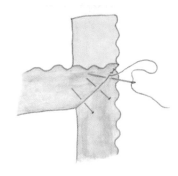

2. On the wrong side, stitch on the pressed line.

3. Trim away any seam allowance and press open.

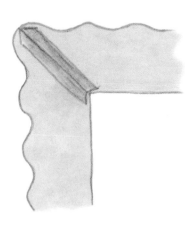

Corner Mitering - Option #2

Use this mitering method on square pieces of cloth such as napkins or on the corner of a drape hem. Practice this a few times and it will become automatic. In the future you won't have to stop and think about it. Don't let a mitered corner stop you. Your home is waiting for you.

1. At the corner to be mitered, turn the seam allowances to the wrong side and press along the seamline.

2. Open flat again and turn back the triangle in the corner of the fabric. Press along the diagonal fold.

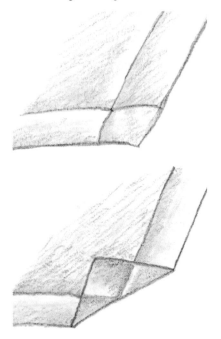

3. Open the corner and fold it diagonally with the wrong sides together. Stitch along the pressed diagonal line.

4. Trim away the seam allowance and press the seam open. Turn the corner to the wrong side. You have a perfect, flat mitered corner.

Trims/Piping/ Cording/Lace

When applying edgings of any sort such as fringe, piping, cording, or ruffles, the rules are basically the same. Most edgings are inserted in a seam, such as around a pillow or the edge of a valance. Almost every photo in this book shows at least one of these edgings somewhere in the room.

Before applying any trims, keep in mind that they can pucker the fabric you are applying them to because of the difference in fabric weights. Always buy a little extra trim so you won't run short. Trims are applied rather loosely and should never be pulled while inserting them in the seam.

Top to bottom: corded tieback, ball fringe, 1″ fringe, lip cording, bullion fringe, tassel fringe, bell tassel off to the side.

Left to right: size 30, size 70, size 150, size 200, 3/8″ cotton piping cord, 1/2″ cotton piping cord, 1″ cotton piping cord.

Where the cord comes together in the seam, you need to do one of three things:

1. If the cord is thin, unravel the ends of the cord and remove a few stitches. These ends will then meet without extra bulk.

2. To bind the cord, twist the ends together and bind it with a needle and thread.

3. Overlap the ends that will be hidden in a deep seam.

When inserting trim in a seam, simply place it on the seam allowance with the raw edges of trim close to the raw edge of fabric. This is the procedure for applying to a 90° turn or a slight curve. Most trims require the use of your zipper foot, but if the trim is flat, you won't need to use it.

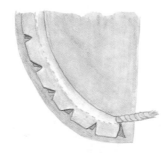

The trim is applied first to one layer of fabric. Instead of pushing the needle right up against the piping, cording, or trim, move it 1/4″ away.

Stitch along the piping but not tight up against it.

When you put the second fabric layer over the trim, have the needle right up against the trim. This way the first line of stitching won't show on the right side. The result speaks for itself.

Stitch close to the trim.

The finished product.

Zipper Insertion

Everyone seems to have their own way of putting in a zipper. If you ever find a way that seems easy to you, use it forever and ever. I personally like the side-lap zipper and find it the quickest and easiest way to get the job done.

1. Sew up the seam allowance using a long stitch and press open.

Press the seam open.

2. Holding the seam allowance together, fold the front seam allowance forward. Using the far seam allowance, fold it to a 1/4″ edge and place the closed zipper behind the 1/4″ narrow edge, with the zipper right side up. The top of the zipper is again on the right.

3. Pin in the narrow edge and out the wide edge (the forward seam allowance).

Tip

Something to memorize for this procedure. "If you take a drink, it will go right to your head." The key word is "right." This means the top of the seam should be in your right hand and the bottom in your left hand.

4. Sewing from the bottom of the zipper with your zipper foot, sew on that narrow edge.

Be sure to stay on the narrow edge.

5. Lay the fabric flat so the zipper io face down on the seam allowance. Sewing from the backside, sew across the bottom of the zipper and up the other side.

Sew across the bottom of the zipper.

6. Sew the remaining side left of the teeth. Use the stitching line on the zipper as a guide. Be sure the fabric doesn't get caught on the front side. Check that it's lying smooth and flat.

Sew the remaining side left of the teeth.

7. Clip the basting stitch that is keeping the flap closed. Presto! A gorgeous zipper every time.

Topstitching

Topstitching can be functional or decorative.

Topstitching is used when you want to emphasize a line of stitching. You can use contrasting threads or color to match.

1. Sew a basic seam and press the seam open.
2. Stitch a line of stitchcs on either side of the seam from the right side.

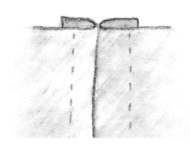

Or press the seam to one side and topstitch only one side.

Buttonholes

Because each sewing machine is different, the best instruction I can give you for buttonholes is to reach for your machine's instruction manual. Practice several buttonholes and they will become a simple task. The beauty of newer sewing machines is that the buttonholes all turn out the same size.

First make a test buttonhole. Check and see if the length is correct.

A test buttonhole.

Check the length.

Sewing With Velcro

Velcro is a quick and easy way to close an opening. Velcro consists of two pieces of material that join hands.

1. To use Velcro, the seam allowance must be wider than the width of the Velcro. Put half of the Velcro on one seam allowance and pin. Sew in place.
2. Place the second half on the other seam allowance, pin, and sew. Be sure to match the alignment of these strips.

Using Machine Feet

This caterpillar has a whole lot of feet to choose from. Knowing which one to choose will make each step go much smoother. This knowledge gives you "good support."

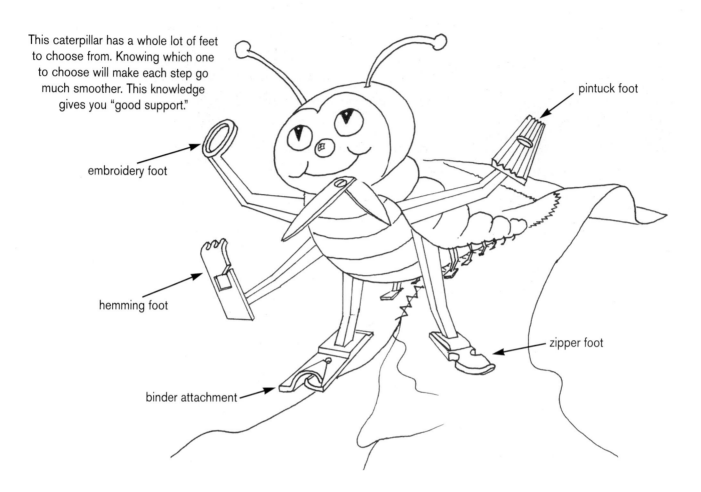

pintuck foot

embroidery foot

hemming foot

zipper foot

binder attachment

There are various feet to help you accomplish a neat hem, ruffle, or binding. There's a walking foot to create even feed, a zipper foot, a narrow hemmer, a seam guide, a buttonhole foot, and quilter's bar.

Combined with the built-in hemming stitch on your machine, the **blindstitch hem foot** positions the hem so you can use this stitch to hem long stretches of fabric. This is especially handy on curtains and bedspreads.

The **ruffler attachment** is a foot that makes it possible to automatically gather strips of fabrics. It's great for making bed ruffles.

The **binder attachment** makes bias binding. This foot folds and attaches bias binding in one step.

The **walking foot** feeds the top and bottom layers of fabric at the same rate. This helps keep plaids and stripes aligned so they will match.

Use the **zipper foot** to insert zippers, cording/piping, fringes, and other trims. The foot can be adjusted to either side of the foot. It helps stitch close to the teeth of the zipper or up next to the trim.

The **narrow hemmer foot** automatically double folds a fabric edge. It's great for hemming napkins (if you don't have a serger).

Attach the **seam guide** to the bed of the machine and adjust it for seam widths up to 1¼".

Use the **buttonhole foot** to make buttonholes. This foot makes it possible to achieve buttonholes that are all the same size. This in itself is a miracle.

A **quilter guide bar** attaches to the foot to form perfectly parallel quilting lines. After you have stitched one row of stitches, the bar rides in that row and keeps the lines straight for the next row.

Use an **embroidery foot** when doing decorative machine stitches.

If you like pintucks, you'll love using a **pintuck foot**. Your pintucks will be evenly spaced and look very professional.

Optional Machine Accessories

New ways to apply ribbon or elastic.

The Ribbon Wizard allows you to stitch three layers of ribbon in one operation with all three layers perfectly lined up. The Ribbon Wizard is a guide that fits on its own metal foot to keep layers of ribbon centered. Up to eight ribbons can be sewn at once.

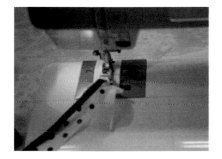

Stitching three layers of ribbon in one operation.

Sewing the elastic right on the seamline.

The Elastic Wizard is a guide that fits on its own metal foot to keep elastic centered. By tightening the screw you can achieve various tensions. You can use the Elastic Wizard with elastic in sizes from 1/8″ to 2″.

The elastic in place.

With a clear understanding of all these machine stitches and various attachments, your home decorating tasks will go faster and smoother. As you practice these techniques, make a notebook of your results so you can refer back to it each time you are called upon to do any of these procedures.

Stitches fill spaces.

CHAPTER EIGHT

Serger Techniques – A Stitch of a Different Kind

I FEEL THAT OWNING A SERGER IS AN HONOR AND A PRIVILEGE. A SERGER HELPS LOWER THE STRESS LEVEL AND MAKES MOST PROJECTS GO MUCH FASTER. YEARS AGO, THE SERGER WAS CALLED AN OVER-LOCK MACHINE. ACCORDING TO SERGER MANUFACTURER BABY LOCK, "SERGING IS A KIND OF KNITTING PROCESS THAT LOOPS TWO, THREE, OR FOUR THREADS TOGETHER TO CREATE A STITCH. THE MACHINE OPERATES WITH ONE OR TWO NEEDLES AND ONE OR TWO LOOPERS, EACH CARRYING A THREAD, THAT TAKE THE PLACE OF A BOBBIN."

A home serger.

An industrial serger.

Serger Tips

Here are some tips that will make using your serger much smoother and less stressful.

❀ **If the stitches skip**: Check your needle. Is it bent, inserted incorrectly, threaded incorrectly? Check the tension.

❀ **If the fabric doesn't feed correctly**: Make sure the presser foot is down. Check the cutting blades to make sure they are sharp. Check the stitch length.

❀ **If the thread breaks**: Make sure the machine is threaded correctly and that the needle is in the machine properly. Check to see if the thread is coming off the spools smoothly.

❀ **If the needle keeps breaking**: First check to see that the machine is correctly threaded. Check for a bent needle. Did you cause the needle to break by pulling the fabric through the machine?

❀ **If the seam is puckered**: Is the machine threaded correctly? Are you using the suggested stitch length? Is the differential feed set properly?

❀ When something goes wrong, first check the way the machine is threaded. I recently spent the better part of a day trying to figure out why my serger thread was breaking. I was sure I had it threaded correctly. In fact, I was positive. Finally, I took out the instruction manual and, lo and behold, I had missed one little hook. After adjusting that, I didn't have any trouble.

Two-Thread, Three-Thread, or Four-Thread?

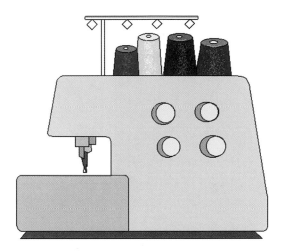

Use the two-thread setting on stretchy fabrics and when overcasting seams, hems, and facings. The left needle creates a wide stitch for heavy and medium weight fabrics and the right needle is best on lightweight fabrics because it is narrower.

Use the three-thread setting for overcasting seams, hems, and facings (same as two-thread for the right and left needle).

Use the four-thread setting on woven fabrics and stable fabrics. This gives you a secure and reinforced seam.

A serged straight edge.

A word about that seemingly complex word *differential*, as in differential feed. What this means is that there are two sets of feed dogs, one in the front and one in the back. They can work independent of each other to give you a smooth seam. (By the way, they don't bark, even though they are feed *dogs*.)

Serging Corners

To serge an **inside corner**, stitch normally until you come to the turn. Stop 1″ from the corner. Lower the needles and raise the presser foot. Manipulate the fabric under the foot by creating a pleat to the left side of the foot. Continue sewing. It doesn't look like an inside corner until you remove it from the machine and unpleat the pleat you created.

For an **outside corner**, stitch to the end of the corner. Stop and raise the needles and the presser foot. Using your fingers or tweezers, pull 1/2″ of thread to create slack. This slack will allow the fabric to be pulled slightly to the back. Turn the fabric, lower the foot, and keep sewing.

Starting and Stopping a Seam

To start a seam:

1. Stitch the seam 1/4″ into the beginning of the fabric.

2. Lower the needles and raise the presser foot.

3. Bring the chain to the front under the foot.

4. Lower the foot and continue sewing while catching the thread chain in the stitches as they form.

To end a seam:

1. Stitch all the way to the end of the seam, but don't go beyond.

2. Stop with the needles up and raise the presser foot.

3. Using your tweezers, pull 1/2″ of slack thread above the needles.

4. Pull the fabric slightly to the rear, clearing the stitches from the stitch fingers.

5. Turn the fabric end over end and position it once again under the presser foot. Lock the knife, lower the presser foot, and stitch again for about 1″ before sewing off the fabric edge.

Stitch normally, then stop 1″ from the turn.

Continue sewing.

Make a pleat in the fabric to the left of the foot.

An example of an inside corner.

A straight outside corner.

Pull to the rear and flip.

Other Serger Capabilities

Gathering on a serger is easy and fast. When gathering large areas like a bed ruffle, the serger will definitely save time. Most serging operations are done with the differential feed set on normal, but for gathering set the differential feed on a smaller number. Use four-thread and start sewing.

As you sew, move the differential feed setting to a lower number.

Gathering on the serger is a fast way to ruffle a long piece of fabric.

Use your serger to make **decorative borders**, quickly finishing off raw edges on tablecloths, napkins, and table runners. You can use an array of threads from fine to heavyweight. Check your manual and thread the loopers and needles for the three-thread setting. You'll love the results. You can create narrow borders, wide borders, or reversible borders.

Narrow hemming is another way to make napkins in a hurry. Use the three-thread and the rolled hem length settings. Stitch around all four sides for napkins that look store bought. Embroider your initials and these napkins will be special in your home.

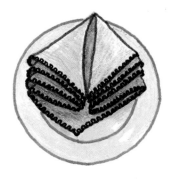

Reconsider investing in a serger for your home. So many people don't buy one because of the fear of threading it. The new sergers are much easier to thread, if not air-threaded for you. I never thought I would say this, but if using the serger to its maximum abilities, you could almost do without a sewing machine altogether. Notice I said *almost*.

CHAPTER NINE

Hand Stitches & Closures

THIS MAY BE THE ONLY BOOK YOU WILL FIND WHERE ALL THE NECESSARY HAND STITCHES ARE ILLUS-
TRATED FOR BOTH RIGHT-HANDED AND LEFT-HANDED STITCHERS. LEFT-HANDERS, YOU WON'T HAVE TO
REVERSE THE STITCH IN YOUR MIND OR IN THE MIRROR OR SIT ACROSS FROM YOUR MOTHER OR
GRANDMOTHER. RIGHT PEOPLE MIGHT BE RIGHT, BUT LEFT PEOPLE SURE AREN'T WRONG. ENJOY THIS
SECTION. I DEDICATE IT TO THE 15% OF THE POPULATION WHO ARE LEFT-HANDED.

STITCHES THE RIGHT-HANDED WAY

Slipstitch

Also called the catch stitch, this stitch is used mainly to join folded edges of fabric together. Use a single thread and be sure to knot the end. Working from right to left, hold the folded edge in your left hand. Bring the needle up through the folded edge and pull the thread out on one edge. Take the next stitch in the opposite edge, directly across from the first stitch, catching only two threads. Pull the needle through and go back to the folded edge. The stitches should be 1/4″ to 1/2″ apart.

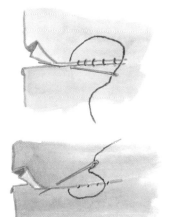

Hemming Stitch

This stitch is great for hemming and can also be decorative. Work from left to right. Knot the end of the thread and catch the knot in the hem edge. At a diagonal angle, catch the hem with a horizontal stitch. Pull the needle through, then catch the fabric

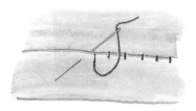

on a diagonal angle again, using a horizontal stitch. Be careful to catch only one or two threads to prevent the stitch from showing on the right side of the fabric.

Tailor Tack

This stitch is used to transfer a pattern mark without using ink or tailor's chalk. Use a double contrasting thread so you will be able to find the marks. Working from right to left, take a 3/8″ length stitch through the fabric. Pull the thread through, leaving a 1″ length of thread on the surface. Insert the needle into the first hole of the stitch again. Take a second stitch through the same holes. Pull the thread through, but leave a loop of tacking thread on the surface. The loop should be about the size of your index finger. After you have completed the markings, gently pull the two layers of fabric apart and snip the threads.

Whipstitch

The whipstitch holds two edges together. It is good for attaching a hook and eye and snaps. The stitches will appear slanted because the nee-

dle is inserted at an angle to the edge. Secure the thread with a fastening stitch through the upper layer of the fabric. With one stitch, catch the fabric edges at the same time. Be careful to catch only one or two threads to prevent the stitch from showing on the right side of the fabric. Stitches should be evenly spaced.

Blanket Stitch

This stitch is also called the buttonhole stitch. This stitch helps neaten the raw edges and also makes a strong edge finish. The buttonhole stitch is worked very closely together and the blanket stitch is spread further apart. Bring the needle up through the material and bring the thread around so it creates a loop. Pull the thread so the caught loop tightens just at the raw edge. If the fabric is heavy, make the stitches wider apart. Bring them closer together for lighter fabrics and very close for a buttonhole.

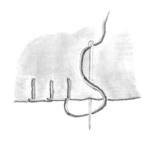

Backstitch

This stitch is used to give strength to a seam. It is meant to be a permanent stitch. This can be used to sew a zipper in by hand or for mending. Working from right to left, push the needle through all the layers of the fabric from the bottom to the top. Insert it again a short distance behind the first stitch. Bring the stitch back out a short distance from where you started. Continue going back and then forward. You are creating stitches that lie on top of each other.

Overcast Stitch

This stitch is used to finish raw edges. By bringing two folded raw edges together, catch the edges on the diagonal and work from right to left.

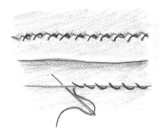

STITCHES THE LEFT-HANDED WAY

Although 15% of the population is left-handed, little is shown the left way when it comes to sewing. When a left-handed person sees a stitch done the "left way," it instantly makes sense. So this is for all you lefties who might be decorating your home (left-handers are known to be creative).

Slipstitch

This stitch is used to hold two layers of fabric together while giving a degree of flexibility. Secure the thread to the top layer of fabric with a fastening stitch. Start at the right; your needle faces the right, but the stitches are moving to the left. This is what causes the thread to cross itself

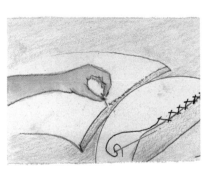

each time. Take a small horizontal stitch in one layer of fabric. Catch one or two threads only. Take another horizontal stitch near the edge of the other layer of fabric. The stitches form a zigzag pattern. Don't pull the stitch too tight and keep the stitches small. End with a backstitch tack.

Hemming Stitch

These are small diagonal stitches taken 1/4″ apart. Secure a single thread with a fastening stitch on the wrong side of the hem. Take your first stitch from the wrong side of the hem edge. Working from left to right, bring the needle up diagonally, catch a few threads of fabric, and come up from the wrong side of the hem edge. The

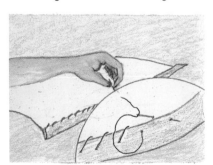

needle should be angled down each time. This produces a series of slanting stitches.

Tailor Tack

For many home sewers, the invention of tracing wheels and colored carbon paper ranks just behind the invention of the sewing machine. Unfortunately, tracing paper has a drawback, one you already know if you have ever mistakenly marked on the right side of your fabric. The marks don't always wash out. Tailor tacks are a time-honored way of reproducing pattern markings. First thread your needle and leave the thread at least 12″ long. No knot is needed. Use a color of thread that contrasts with the fabric. (A great place to use leftover thread.) With the pattern still pinned to the fabric, insert the needle down through the pattern and fabric, then back up again 1/2″ - only once. Hold up the long ends of the thread and cut them off long. Do each pattern marking in the same manner. As you finish each section, unpin the pattern. Then carefully pull the tissue off the fabric and cut the threads between the two fabric pieces. The right-handed way is described differently. I have found that this way is easier for us lefties.

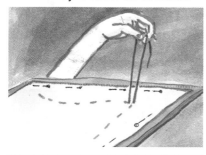

Whipstitch

The whipstitch holds two edges together. It is good for attaching a hook and eye, and snaps. The stitches will appear slanted because the needle is inserted at a right angle to the edge. Secure the thread with a fastening stitch through the upper layer of the fabric. With one stitch,

catch the fabric edges at the same time. Be careful to catch only one or two threads to prevent the stitch from showing on the right side of the fabric. Stitches should be evenly spaced.

Blanket Stitch

This stitch is done on the raw edge of fabric but to get the rhythm of the stitch, do it on the fabric as shown first. Mark the fabric with one line to show the upper extension of the stitches and another line to show the baseline (this could also be the edge of the fabric). Beginning on the right, bring the needle through to the front of the fabric at the end of the baseline, holding down the thread with your right thumb while you insert the needle into the top guideline a little to the left. Bring it through to the front again, directly below on the baseline, or under the edge of the fabric. (In binding a raw edge, the needle will enter the fabric only on the top guidoline.) Pull through, making sure the needle is over the loop of thread and catches it. Continue working to the left.

Backstitch

Starting on the left, bring the needle and thread to the top layer of the pieces being sewn. Insert the needle through all fabric layers 1/8″ behind the point where the thread emerges.

Bring the needle and thread out the same distance beyond the point where the thread first emerged. Continue this pattern, being sure the needle and thread are a half stitch length behind and beyond the thread from the previous stitch.

Overcast Stitch

Overcast stitches are diagonal over the edge. Secure the thread with a fastening stitch on the wrong side of the fabric. Hold the needle straight up and down, perpendicular to the fabric. Insert the needle on the wrong side of the fabric. The thread will go around the edge with each stitch. Stitches are 1/4″ apart. Finish with a backstitch tack.

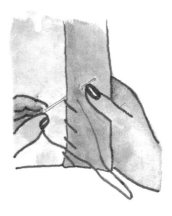

I hope by illustrating these stitches the left-handed and right-handed way, there will be an equal number of left-handers and right-handers who will be able to sew a beautiful home.

CLOSURES

Snaps

Through my years of teaching sewing, I have discovered that there are many ways to sew on snaps - ways that one would never think of. But there really is a right and wrong way. So let's make them look neat. Snaps are small fasteners with less strength than hooks and eyes. Use them on overlapping edges where there won't be much strain.

A snap consists of two parts: a ball and a socket. Snaps range in size from 4 (heavy-duty) to 0 (lightweight). The ball half is sewn on the wrong side of the upper layers, the socket half is sewn on the right side of the lower layer. Place the ball half on the wrong side of the overlap, making sure it is far enough in from the edge to not show. In the ball half, whipstitch over each hole and carry the thread under the snap when going from hole to hole.

To mark the location of the socket half, rub tailor's chalk on the ball, position the closing, and apply pressure. Center the socket on the transferred mark. Start with the left hole and work from left to right.

Hooks & Eyes

Hooks and eyes are used when there will be strain on the closing. General purpose hooks and eyes come in sizes 0 (fine) to 3 (heavy). They come in black or nickel finishes. Although hooks and eyes are small, they are very strong. There are two types of eyes available: the bar eye and the curved eye.

Use the bar eye when the two pieces of fabric being joined will overlap. Place the eye on the right side of the lower layer and the hook on the wrong side of the upper layer. Sew the hook on first, using a whipstitch, and secure it with a fastening stitch. The hook should be 1/8″ from the edge of the upper layer. Using the whipstitch, pass the needle and thread through the fabric around the circular holes. Don't forget to sew down the extension of the hook so it will lie against the fabric. Sew a few stitches around the farthest flat part of the hook through one fabric layer only. This will hold it securely in place but not show on the outside. Mark on the lower layer where the end of the hook will fall. Whipstitch the bar eye in place by passing the needle and thread through each hole, from left to right. Secure the thread.

Use the curved eye when the two pieces of fabric will butt against each other. Place both the hook and eye on the wrong side of the garment. The method of attaching them is the same as with the bar eye, but the hook should be placed 1/16″ from the edge, and the eye should be placed so it extends slightly beyond the edge.

Use a straight eye when the two sides overlap.

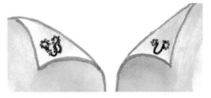

Use a round eye when the two sides meet exactly.

Buttons

When sewing on two- or four-hole buttons, bring the needle up from the bottom and take your stitches horizontally, vertically, or as Xs. Whichever you decide, be consistent.

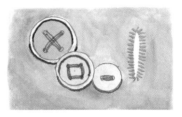

Fabric-Covered Buttons

In some cases, you'll want to use fabric-covered buttons instead of those you buy ready to use. When covering buttons, take time to decide on the center of the design. You can cover buttons with contrasting fabrics to create a decorative look or matching fabric for a subtle effect. Fabric-covered buttons are especially effective on cushions.

The quickest and easiest way to cover buttons is to buy a covered button kit that includes the metal button shell, a back, a pusher, and a rubber button maker. Cut the fabric to size using the pattern included on the package or twice the diameter of the button. Center the fabric, wrong side up, and the button shell over the button maker and push into the button maker. Tuck the fabric and use the pusher to snap the back into the shell. Success almost every time.

Stitches fill spaces.

CHAPTER TEN

One Room, Six Styles

Style means many things to many people. Style refers to a period or region. When you achieve a certain style, you recognize certain traits and characteristics that remind you of that region. When something is actually stylish, it takes on a whole new meaning. Something is stylish when the elements of design are put together and you gain pleasure from it. It is this pleasure you are trying to achieve. After all, in your home you want to feel positive and comfortable. Decorating is a process towards an end - it is not a product. It is through this process that you turn your house into a home.

We took six photographs of the same room, using the same sofa, chair, and end table to illustrate how changing only the accessories can change the style. Not only does the style change - so does the ambiance. Keep in mind that you have the right to mix and match any of these styles. You might like country in your kitchen but would prefer something more traditional in the living room. Remember - there are no wrong decisions. This is your home. The ultimate goal is to sew a beautiful home - your home.

Starting with neutral furniture gives you the option to change the accessories as often as you like. Neutral colors in a room create a tranquil environment.

First decide what overall effect you want in your room. Here are some quick ideas that will give you certain styles - and ambiance.

Victorian Style. For a romantic or Victorian style, use fresh colors such as ivory, peach, and pastel pink. The Victorian period covered the time during Queen Victoria's reign (1837-1901). Furniture tends to be heavy and massive in size. Black walnut, rosewood, and mahogany were often used. Choose fabrics such as polished cottons, velvets, brocades, satins, silks, florals, laces, and eyelet borders. Incorporate baby dolls dressed in period costume. A canopy bed with white lace trimmed bed linens would be the icing on the romantic cake. Add a scarf, vintage hat, trays, and fans.

Contemporary Style. For a contemporary style, choose neutral tones such as beige, gray, ivory, and cream. Select fabrics that have texture with simple designs. Add animal print fabrics to the mixture. This particular style ends up being very strong and sleek. Don't be afraid to mix some old furniture with new furniture. Add some modern art pieces and a glass table.

Oriental Style. For an oriental style, try using a sliding screen, dark wood furniture, and oriental accessories such as the vase, pillows, and picture on the wall. The use of black and cream prints would also be a wise choice. Other effective touches are Oriental rugs, Oriental art, strong colors, and bamboo.

English Country Style. For an English country style, your mental image is usually a country setting with a comfortable room and a roaring fire in the background. Fabrics often used include florals or chintzes with stenciled walls, quilts, and lots of pastels. The English country look also blends Shaker-style furniture mixed with accessories such as a spinning wheel, tinware, baskets, country style fishing baskets, straw hats with ribbon bands, rag rugs, wooden boxes, and crocks.

Right: The Beach Look. For a cheerful look, as in a beach house, use bright colors such as green, orange, blue, and yellow, otherwise known as cool colors. Select fabrics with stripes and bold florals. Decorator cotton prints are readily available.

Below right: Southwestern Style. To accomplish the southwestern style, consider using bandannas, Western pictures, cowboy hats, and pillows made with southwestern prints. Southwestern also includes Mexican blankets, terra cotta planters, horse tack, boots, and pottery.

Of course, there are many more styles than the ones pictured. Always popular is the **traditional style**, with reliable colors such as white, blue, burgundy, and green. Select fabrics such as jacquards, matelasses, linens, velvets, and satins and incorporate tassels on the drapes and Impressionist paintings on the walls.

The **eclectic style** combines four to six different patterns in the same room. Be careful, if you overdo this, your room can end up looking like a hodgepodge. Use color to pull this style together. Add a maple desk, glass-top coffee table, mirrors with gold frames, and brass pots and you have eclectic.

For a **cozy look**, use medium hues such as mauve, green, and blue. Choose quilted fabrics or ones that have small prints. A cozy room is a great place to use chintzes and satins.

For a **masculine look**, use lots of earth tones. Here is where you can use browns, rusts, blues, and greens and plaid or striped fabrics.

As your own decorator, you have so many options. Along with choosing accessories you can choose designs, colors, window treatments, floor plans, a mountain of fabrics, and your family's personal preferences. This thought should keep you going.

Style fills space.

CHAPTER ELEVEN
Filling Spaces With Pillows

Pillows fill spaces and add color and style to any setting.
Bottom row: oblong flange, bolster with fringe, envelope pillow.
Second row: oblong with ruffle and 1/4″ welt. Third row:
square corded pillow, oblong with fringe, square corded, square
with ball fringe.
Top row: square with fringe, two-tone oblong with cording,
square two-tone with rope trim.

IMAGINE YOUR BEDROOM, LIVING ROOM, OR ANY ROOM WITHOUT PILLOWS. YOU MAY FIND IT DIFFICULT, EVEN IMPOSSIBLE TO IMAGINE, BUT DOING SO MAKES YOU REALIZE VERY QUICKLY THE IMPORTANCE OF PILLOWS. BASICALLY, PILLOWS FILL BLANK SPACES AND ADD COLOR AND STYLE TO ANY ROOM.

PILLOWS ARE SOFT AND SAFE. PILLOWS CAN BE ANY SIZE OR SHAPE, FANCY, FIRM, OR SQUISHY. THEY CAN BE CUTE, COMFORTABLE, OR JUST PLAIN PRACTICAL. IF YOU HAVE DECIDED ON A STYLE, PILLOWS GIVE MERIT TO YOUR CHOICE. FOR EXAMPLE, COUNTRY PILLOWS CAN HAVE RUFFLES, APPLIQUÉS, QUILTED PIECES, AND COMBINATIONS OF SCRAPS. WITH A LITTLE THOUGHT, YOU CAN CLEVERLY MIX AND MATCH PILLOW FABRICS TO GIVE A ROOM A WHOLE NEW LOOK. PILLOWS ARE THE PERFECT DEVICES TO DRAW A WHOLE HOME DECORATING SCHEME TOGETHER.

GINGHAM WAS KNOWN IN THE PAST AS THE FABRIC OF CHOICE FOR PILLOWS, BUT ALL FABRICS ARE FAIR GAME FOR PILLOWS. CHECK OUT FAUX SUEDE, VELVET, MOHAIR, AND OTHER TEXTURED FABRICS. EVERYONE KNOWS THAT BUYING A NEW PAIR OF SHOES OR A NEW PURSE UPDATES AN OLD OUTFIT. THE SAME IS TRUE FOR PILLOWS. THERE IS NO SIMPLER WAY TO KEEP ROOMS CURRENT AT A RELATIVELY LOW COST THAN TO ADD PILLOWS. YOU DESERVE TO SURROUND YOURSELF IN THE COMFORT AND LUXURY OF BEAUTIFUL PILLOWS IN YOUR BEAUTIFUL HOME. (REFER TO CHAPTER TEN "ONE ROOM, SIX STYLES" AND NOTICE HOW PILLOWS CHANGE THE STYLE.)

PILLOW FILLINGS

The expression, "It's what's inside that counts," is true when referring to pillows. For the pillow to look neat on the outside, some thought needs to go into choosing the filling. Pillows get their shape from the filling and there are many types of filling available.

Down

If you have ever owned a goose-filled pillow, you already know the advantages of using this as a filling. Down comes from the breasts of geese and ducks. The disadvantage to down is that it is expensive, but it allows body moisture to evaporate quickly. In this case "down" is a good thing.

Kapok

This filling, a vegetable fiber filling, is very soft. It gives a nice finished pillow but is messy to work with. It can also tend to become lumpy and it is not at all washable.

Fiberfill

This can be made from polyester or acrylic and is completely washable, even after it has been packed in the fabric casing. Fiberfill is inexpensive and allergy-free. You can buy pre-sewn fiberfill pillow forms in all the basic shapes (round, square, rectangular) or you can buy loose fiberfill. The forms range from 10″ to 30″.

Foam

Foam comes in sheets, blocks, and chips. Sheets of foam are available in thicknesses of 1/2″ to 5″. Cutting the foam can be rather tricky so you might want to ask the sales-

Pillows get their shape from what's inside and there are many fillings to choose from. Left to right: down, kapok, fiberfill, foam filling, foam blocks.

person to cut a piece for you. If you cut it yourself, use a serrated knife with silicone lubricant sprayed on the blade.

Foam chips are used to stuff a pre-sewn pillow cover. There is no doubt it is resilient but it has a tendency to become lumpy.

Foam blocks are your best choice for seat cushions. They are resilient and bounce right back after you sit on them. Foam blocks can be cut in any shape.

The charts on page 73 will make it easy for you to determine how much fabric you need for various pillow sizes.

Different names are used for different pillow sizes. For example, a 12″ x 16″ pillow is called a boudoir pillow, a 6″ x 14″ a neck roll or bolster, and a 26″ x 26″ a European square. The

standard bed pillow is 20″ x 26″, queen is 20″ x 30″, and king is 20″ x 36″.

After you decide on the filling for the pillow, you can decide what kind of pillow to add to that special room. Remember: pillows fill spaces. Pillows can be simple or elaborate. If you are a beginning sewer, start with a square or round pillow to give you confidence. Then work up to ruffled pillows, flange pillows, corded pillows, and bolsters.

Decide on the closure next. Perhaps you want to whipstitch the seam closed by hand, or add a zipper, use Velcro, buttons, snap tape, or ties. Review "Closures" on page 66 and choose the one that's easiest for you. Pillow making can be addictive, so be prepared. In fact, pillows and rabbits have something in common - they multiply quickly.

Round Pillows	Yardage Amount
	(45″ or 54″-wide)
12″-14″	1 yd.
16″-18″	1¼ yds.
20″-24″	1⅝ yds.

Square Pillows	Yardage Amount	
	45″-wide	54″-wide
12″ sq.	1/2 yd.	1/2 yd.
14″ sq.	1/2 yd.	1/2 yd.
16″ sq.	1/2 yd.	1/2 yd.
18″ sq.	5/8 yd.	5/8 yd.
20″ sq.	5/8 yd.	5/8 yd.
24″ sq.	1½ yds.	3/4 yd.
30″ sq.	1¾ yds.	2 yds.

Pillow Shams	Yardage Amount (54″ wide)		
	Regular	Queen	King
Flange	2¼ yds.	2¼ yds.	2¼ yds.
Ruffled	3¼ yds.	3¼ yds.	3½ yds.
Corded	1¾ yds.	2¼ yds.	2¼ yds.

KNIFE-EDGE PILLOW

The best place to start when beginning to make pillows is a basic knife-edge pillow, also referred to as a liner. You can use the knife-edge pillow as the filling for a decorative cover, or you can sew it with decorative fabric and use it as a pillow on its own. Knife-edge pillows are quick and easy to make and shouldn't take longer than an hour. Use muslin, a firm woven cotton or cotton blend, cotton sateen, or sheeting.

The pink pillows and aqua pillows are knife-edge pillows. The white ones are knife-edge pillows with fringe. The two bed pillows in the back are covered with decorative shams.

To make an envelope pillow from a basic knife-edge, simply add a hemmed triangle of fabric to one side.

Materials

To make a 16" square knife-edge pillow

* 16" pillow form
* 1/2 yd. fabric (45" or wider) Allow extra for a print that needs centering.
* 3/8 yd. contrasting fabric for the flap (by adding this you create an envelope pillow)
* 2 yd. fringe if desired
* Thread to match

Instructions:

1. Cut two pieces of fabric the length and width of the pillow form, centering the design if necessary and adding 1/2" seam allowances on all the edges.

2. If you want to create an envelope pillow, cut two triangles of contrasting or matching fabric, seam it, turn and press, and sew it on the top edge of the cut fabric, matching the seam allowances.

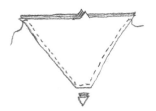

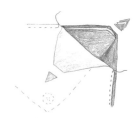

Adding a triangle on one side to create an envelope pillow.

3. If using fringe, sew the fringe around the main piece of fabric at this time.

4. Right sides together, stitch around all the edges, leaving an opening on the bottom edge to turn the pillow right side out.

leave open

5. For a corner that won't seem floppy (or dog-eared), instead of making a 90° turn at the corner, mark 1/2" from the corner and up the sides 1/2". As you sew around the corner, sew a semi-curve rather than a sharp corner.

6. Trim the corners if it is square and clip the curves if it is round.

7. Turn the pillow cover to the outside and press.

8. nsert the pillow form and slip-stitch the opening closed. If you need to fill out the corners you can place a little fiberfill in each corner to give a nice crisp corner.

By just adding a decorative rope tie with a tassel, the room takes on a whole new look and so does the pillow.

Refer to "Trims/Piping/Cording/Lace" on page 53 for ways to add cording/piping or ruffles. Consider a zipper or Velcro as a closure (see Closures on page 66).

This elegant knife-edge pillow is made from French silk fabric and features ties from multi-colored silk rope and a double tassel.

This square pillow features a tight ruffle lace, and mitered 90° corners.

MOCK TURKISH PILLOW

This is a pillow that is a lot of fun to make and certainly will impress your guests. They will think you worked hours to accomplish this. Turkish pillows are certain to be a success because cording is unnecessary. Very large Turkish pillows make great floor cushions, medium-size ones will transform a bed into a sofa, and smaller pillows can be used as color accents on a bed or sofa. The shape of a Turkish pillow can be square or rectangular.

Materials:

To make a 16″ pillow
* 1/2 yd. fabric (45″ or wider)
* Fiberfill or 16″ pillow form
* String or dental floss
* Thread to match

Instructions:

1. Using the directions for the knife-edge pillow, make and sew a square or rectangular pillow cover.

2. After the seams are sewn, mark a pencil line across each corner at an angle.

3. Tie the corners with string or dental floss and turn the pillow right side out. The corners are now inside and they create a mock Turkish corner.

4. Fill the pillow and slipstitch the opening closed or consider using snaps.

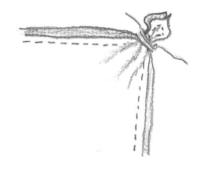

TRAPUNTO PILLOW

Here's another interesting pillow. Trapunto is found in boutiques where satin, suede, and UltraSuede vests and jackets are embroidered and padded. A simpler form of trapunto is seen when an appliqué is stitched to a pair of jeans and stuffed with poly fiberfill before stitching is completed. Another form of trapunto, called Italian quilting, is used on sofa cushions where a raised design is created by drawing a cord through stitched channels.

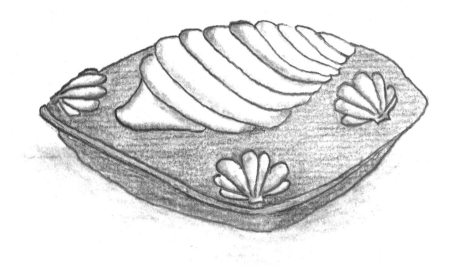

Trapunto is a quilting technique where a design is stitched through two layers of fabric. The bottom layer (the backing) is slit and padding is inserted to raise the design. The outside layer of fabric might be a graphic textile or a lightweight printed fabric such as a large floral print or an animal print.

Materials:

To make a 16″ pillow

* 1/2 yd. fabric with a printed design (45″ or wider)
* 16″ square of lining or sheeting x 2
* Fiberfill
* Thread to match

Instructions:

1. Cut the backing layer of lightweight fabric (not knit) the same size as the decorative fabric. An old sheet will work nicely for the backing.
2. For padding, use fiberfill sold in pound bags. Pin the backing layer to the wrong side of the outside layer. No need to baste, just pin.
3. With the outside layer up, machine stitch around the parts of the design you want to raise.
4. Turn the backing side up. Carefully snip holes in the backing in the area to be raised, taking care not to cut through the outside fabric layer. Push the fiberfill through the slits, with the eraser end of a pencil. Make sure to fill all areas, including the small areas. Slipstitch or whipstitch the slits closed.

NO-SEW PILLOW

If you're one of those people who would rather not sew, this no-sew pillow is for you. This is a great way to give new life to an old or stained pillow. A fun fast way to create holiday pillows.

Materials:

To make a 16" pillow
* 16" pillow form (or any pillow that needs re-covered)
* 1¼ yds. fabric (45" or wider)
Note: It's best to use reversible fabric.
* Rubber band

Instructions:

1. Measure a square pillow and cut a square twice that size out of your fabric of choice. In this case, cut a 45" square.
2. Place your pillow in the middle of the fabric on the diagonal.
3. Bring the four corners up over the pillow, towards the center and secure with a rubber band.
4. Create a flower or rosette by tucking the excess fabric under the rubber band. Like magic, you have a newly decorated pillow. You can also tie it with a cord and tassel, or wired ribbon for those special occasions.

Tip

Consider using a lace dresser scarf or other antique scarf to re-cover an old pillow.

BOLSTER PILLOW

Bolsters are also called neck rolls. They are often trimmed with lace, ruffles, buttons, piping, and tassels. They look great on a bed or chair. If you have a teenager who loves to lay on the sofa and watch TV, you might want to throw one of these pillows on the sofa. This could be a problem though - he or she may become too comfortable!

Above: The denim bolster is the perfect accent piece for this yellow and blue bed decor.

Right: The regal bolster in the front of this grouping is fit for a king.

You'll need approximately 3/4 yd. of 45″-wide fabric, a bolster form (readily available in your fabric store), and the trim of choice.

A bolster can have cording at the ends, fringe around each end, or perhaps have a tied end. A bolster can also be very plain. For a simple, unadorned bolster, follow these simple steps.

Materials:

※ Bolster pillow form
※ 3/4 yd. fabric (45″ or wider)
※ Thread to match

Instructions:

1. Cut one piece of fabric 20″ x 15″. Trace the round end of the bolster form and cut two, adding 1/2″ seam allowances.

2. Fold the large piece of fabric in half crosswise and stitch the edges, leaving an opening. Use 1/2″ seam allowances.

3. Stitch the round circles on each end. Trim the seams.

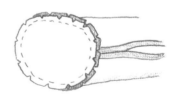

4. Turn right side out, insert the form, and close the opening using a slipstitch.

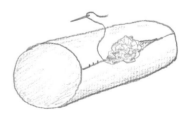

RUFFLED BOLSTER

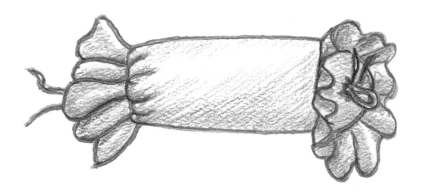

Materials:

* Bolster pillow form
* 1 yd. of fabric (45″ or wider)
* 1½ yds. ribbon
* 1⅜ yds. piping
* Thread to match

Instructions:

1. Cut one piece of fabric 20″ x 15″. Cut two end pieces that measure 3½″ x 20″. Cut four ruffle pieces each 7″ x 28″.

2. Stitch the piping to the short ends of the main piece. Fold the long sides together crosswise (right sides) and stitch 1/4″ seams.

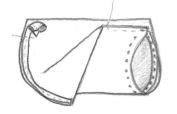

3. Make a ruffle or use purchased lace and stitch it on the ends of the main piece. With right sides together, sew the end pieces.

4. Make a casing on the edge of these last pieces by turning the edge under 1/4″. Press and turn under another 1/2″. Stitch.

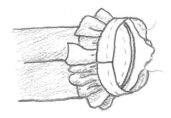

5. Pull a ribbon or drawstring through the casing using a safety pin or Fasturn. Knot and tie.

HEART-SHAPED PILLOW

A heart-shaped pillow is great in a girl's room. This would be a great project to do together. Let her pick out the lace and help sew the seams. This is also a great gift idea.

You'll need approximately 1/2 yd. of fabric 45″ or wider, pillow filling, and three yards of eyelet trim. Buying the lace already gathered saves time.

Materials:

To make a 14″ heart-shaped pillow
* 1/2 yd. fabric (45″ or wider)
* Poly fiberfill
* 1½ yds. gathered eyelet trim
* Thread to match

Instructions:

1. Use those skills you learned in first grade to cut a heart shape out of paper. Cut two pieces of fabric using the paper pattern, adding 1/2″ seam allowances.

2. Gather the lace.

3. Pin the gathered lace to the right side of one of the fabric hearts.

4. Right sides together, place the other fabric heart over the first half and stitch all layers, being sure to catch the lace in the stitching. Leave a small opening to turn the pillow.

5. Trim the seams.

6. Turn the pillow right side out, stuff with filling, and slipstitch the opening.

Tip
Imagine this pillow made in miniature for a little girl's favorite doll.

FLANGE PILLOW

A flange is actually a flat border around a knife-edge pillow. The flange is usually 2″ wide and can be single or double. This flange pillow is for a standard size bed pillow.

The flange on this pillow is made with contrasting fabric.

The center pillow in red brocade and the two white pillows arc flange pillows.

You'll need approximately 2 yds. of fabric 45″ or wider.

Materials:

* Standard bed pillow
* 2 yds. fabric (45″ or wider)
* Thread to match

Instructions:

1. Cut one rectangle 32″ x 26″ (includes 1/2″ seam allowance). Cut two pieces for the back that measure 22″ x 26″ (includes 1/2″ seam allowance). These measurements provide for a 4″ overlap and a 1/2″ hem allowance.

2. Turn under the short edges of the two back pieces 1/2″ and hem. These hemmed edges will form the opening on the back of the pillow and actually overlap.

3. With right sides together, stitch the two back pieces to the front piece, overlapping the two back pieces as shown. Trim the seams.

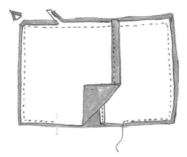

4. Turn right side out and press. Mark 2″ in from the outside edge and stitch.

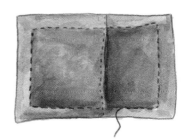

5. Insert the pillow through the opening in the back.

FLANGE PILLOW VARIATION

A flange pillow can also be made in separate pieces. The outside edge is made from a separate piece of fabric and sewn to the pillow panels.

Materials:

To make an 18″ pillow
- 14″ pillow form
- 2 yds. fabric (45″ or wider)
- 1 yd. cording
- Thread to match

Instructions:

1. Cut one 14″ square, adding a 1/2″ seam allowance. Cut two pieces for the back that measure 18″ x 12″, adding a 1/2″ seam allowance. Cut four strips of fabric that measure 3″ by 22″ (the excess can be trimmed later, it's better to have too much than not enough).

2. If you decide on cording, stitch the cording around the 14″ square using the zipper foot. Where the cords come together, twist them and stitch in place.

Stitching on the cording.

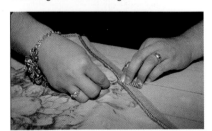

A cording joint.

3. Pin a fabric strip to the corded edge. Break your stitching at each corner.

4. To miter the corners, fold under the overlapped banding to create a

45° angle. It is best to baste the corners at this point to make sure they lay flat.

5. Stitch the strips together using the pressed edge as a guide. Trim the excess fabric from the seam of the mitered corner.

6. Baste the corners to the pillow front and stitch all four corners, making sure the seam is aligned with each corner edge.

The edge made up of the mitered strips is now sewn to the inner square.

7. Turn under the long edges of the two back pieces and hem. These hemmed edges will form the opening on the back of the pillow and actually overlap.

A mock flange pillow is possible when using a border print. Stitching around the border will give you a flange look.

8. Stitch the two back pieces to the completed front piece using 1/2″ seam allowances. Clip at the corner so you will have sharp edges when it is turned.

9. Insert the pillow form.

Inserting the pillow form in the flange cover.

BOX-EDGE PILLOW

Another very common pillow is the box-edge pillow. This can be a throw pillow or can lead to projects like seat cushions and sofa cushions. The principles are the same. This pillow has three pieces - a front, back, and side (commonly called a boxing strip). You can add cording, ruffles, or other trims to dress it up.

Notice the boxing strips on the sides of this pillow.

Materials:

* 1 yd. fabric (45″ or wider)
* Fiberfill
* Thread to match

Instructions:

1. Measure the length and width of the pillow form. Cut out the front and back to these measurements, adding 1/2″ seam allowances.

2. Using the total length and width of the pillow, cut the boxing strip pieces to that measurement plus 1/2″ seam allowances. If you have to piece the strip, add 1″ to the total length for each seam. Sew the short ends of the long strip together.

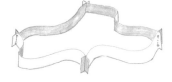

3. Mark four cuts on the strip after lining it up on the front piece of the pillow in all four corners. With right sides together, pin and stitch the front to the boxing strip.

4. Stitch the back of the pillow to the other edge of the boxing strip, matching up the corners. Leave a small opening for turning.

5. Trim or clip the seams and turn right side out. Insert the pillow form and slipstitch the opening.

ROUND PILLOW

Read through the instructions for making a knife-edge pillow on page 73. Add a boxing strip and you will have a round fitted box-edge pillow.

Materials:

❋ Round foam pillow form (or cut a round from a square foam form)
❋ 1 yd. fabric (45″ or wider)
❋ 1¾ yds. cording/trim/piping (optional)
❋ Thread to match

Instructions:

1. Measure the diameter of the pillow and cut out two circles of fabric, adding 1/2″ seam allowances.

2. Measure around the outside of the pillow form to determine the length of the boxing strip. Cut a piece of fabric this length by the depth of the pillow plus a 1/2″ seam allowance. You may have to piece the strip to achieve the length you need.

3. If using trim, stitch it on the right side of one of the fabric circles.

4. Right sides together, stitch the boxing strip to the first fabric circle. Place the second fabric circle over the boxing strip, right sides together, and stitch in place. Leave an opening for turning and inserting the pillow form.

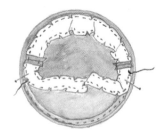

5. Turn right side out, insert the pillow form, and slipstitch the opening.

Tip

If you can't find a round pillow form, you can change a square one to round by punching in the corners.

TUFTED PILLOW

Button tufting on a pillow not only looks nice but the button keeps the filling inside the pillow from shifting. Obviously, this means the cover won't be removable for cleaning. To sew buttons on pillows or cushions, you will need a large upholstery needle and strong thread. This tufted pillow is often made like the box-edge knife pillow or the round box pillow. Refer to the instructions on page 73. Tufting can be done on any pillow.

Materials:

* Covered pillow
* Long upholstery needle
* Upholstery thread or dental floss
* Two buttons (1″ or larger)

Instructions:

1. Thread a long upholstery needle with extra-strong thread.
2. Thread strands through the button shank and tie with a double knot.
3. Push the needle through the pillow and pull the button tight against the pillow.

Pull the button tight against the pillow.

Inserting the needle.

4. Thread the second button on the reverse side of the pillow, using only one strand of thread. Tie the two strands so the button is pulled tight against the pillow.
5. Wrap the thread a few times around the button shank, tie a double knot, and trim the threads.

Tightening the button.

Filled spaces are a necessary ingredient in any beautiful home. When pillows look inviting, you will find people filling spaces.

Pillows fill spaces.

CHAPTER TWELVE

Window Treatments

CURTAINS QUICKLY ADD DRAMA TO ANY WINDOW. WHEN PLANNING A WINDOW
TREATMENT, YOUR GOAL IS TO ENHANCE THE WINDOW WITHOUT DOMINATING IT.
LARGE WINDOWS CAN BE MADE TO LOOK SMALLER AND SMALL WINDOWS CAN BE
MADE TO LOOK LARGER - ALL BY SELECTING THE RIGHT STYLE, FABULOUS FABRIC, AND
HARDWARE FOR THE WINDOW TREATMENT.

SELECTING A STYLE

When deciding on the style of window treatment for your room, look through magazines and books to give you ideas. Spend a couple hours at your local bookstore. There are so many styles to choose from and so many ways to decorate a window. It is truly a matter of taste. Specialty drapery hardware makes it possible to simply drape your fabric to achieve decorative window fashions such as swags and jabots (cascades).

Just to give you an idea, here are some examples:

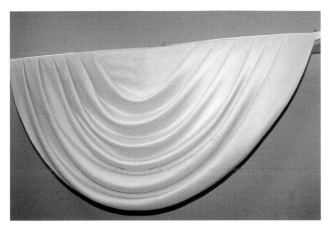

Pleated swag.

Pleated swag with a standard cascade.

Single swag with fringe.

A banded valance with cutouts.

SELECTING A STYLE

A cloud shade with a ruffled bottom.

Roman shades made from multi-colored cotton.

A draped swag with balloon sheers. (Yes, you can see me in the mirror - hard at work.)

A striped stagecoach shade with gingham ties.

SELECTING A STYLE

A woven Aztec stagecoach shade with contrast straps.

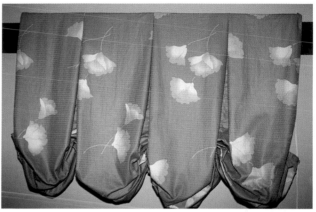

An inverted box pleat balloon shade.

A purchased shirring tape header with a double ruffle balloon shade.

A rod pocket shaped valance on a Continental rod, with a separate coordinating balloon shade.

SELECTING A STYLE

Button-back curtains.

A draped swag with rosettes.

Puddle curtains with rosettes.

A triple swag with cascades.

SELECTING A STYLE

A damask striped tab curtain on a wooden rod.

A padded cornice board draped with a silk/rayon blend swag.

A triple swag drape with stacked cascades and a Maltese cross rosette.

HARDWARE

Selecting the proper drapery hardware is as important as choosing the right fabric for your curtains. Since you should mount the hardware before measuring the windows for fabric, the hardware decision comes early in the game. Refer to Chapter Six for how to measure the window.

Decorative Poles & Rods

An assortment of rods, finials, and tie backs.

Top to bottom: wood poles and accessories shown in brown and white, a decorator pole set, and a traditional café rod for shirred-on curtains with a 1½″ rod pocket or pleated panels.

There is no shortage of decorative poles and rods and finials in today's stores. These can be made from wood (natural or painted), brass, and iron and are used only when the span is straight (not curved). The width of the pole should be able to support the weight of the fabric. If the span is wide, be sure to use a bracket in the middle to support the weight of the curtains.

In addition to decorator poles, other simple hanging systems include:

Spring Wire or Sash Rods

These are the simplest to mount - you just let the spring tension create the pressure necessary to hold the rod in place. They are also the least stable and should be used for lightweight curtains. They feature a soft rubber tip on each end and the spring-tension rods can extend to fit various widths. These are great for shower curtains.

Top to bottom: three single curtain rods with varying returns and a sash rod.

Single Curtain Rods

These are used for rod pocket curtains and stationary window treatments. They can be purchased in colors or clear so the rod won't show when inserted in the fabric. Clear rods are wonderful for sheer and lace curtains. You can also paint the rods to coordinate with your fabric.

Double Curtain Rods

These consist of two rods with 1″ difference in the clearance to hang a valance and a curtain on the same mounting.

2½″ and 4½″ Rods

These wide curtain rods are available in 2½″ and 4½″ depths. They add emphasis at the top of a curtain and add depth to the rod pockets of shirred curtains. Great for bay windows and corner windows. The connectors make it possible for you to sew a continuous window treatment. You will have only one window treatment per rod. If you use a Dauphine™ rod, you will have two window treatments for the 2½″ rod and one window treatment on the 4½″ rod.

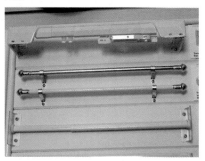

Top to bottom: a traverse rod, a traditional café rod, a spring pressure rod, and a 4½″ curtain rod.

Traverse Rods

Traverse rods are used for draperies that open and close with a pull cord. The draperies hide the rods when the panels are closed. These can open from the center or from either side.

You can also find decorative traverse rods where the draperies are attached to rings that slide on a hidden track. With these, you won't need a top treatment because the rods are decorative - usually brass or wood finished.

Accessories

Tieback hooks and clasps are available in both simple and elaborate designs. These hold the curtains open.

The rod or pole you select will determine the curtain rod pocket size. The chart below will help you identify the proper size of the rod pocket.

Type of Rod	Rod Pocket for Sheers	Rod Pocket for Lightweight Cotton
1″ curtain or tension rod	1½″	1½″
3/4″ round pole	1½″	2″
1″ round pole	2″	2½″
2″ round pole	3¾″	3¾″
4½″	5½″	5½″

PLEATER TAPES

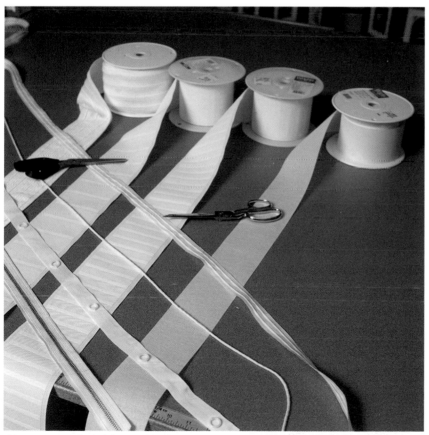

You can save yourself a lot of time by using pleater tapes. These handy tapes have pockets that create perfect sized pleats (or gathers). It is best to start and end with an unpleated space. To figure the exact amount of pleater tape needed, buy the amount equal to the cutting width of both drapes plus four extra spaces. If the drapes have a two-way draw, buy eight extra spaces.

Pleater tapes left to right: spools of transparent pinch pleater tape, 3⅞″ regular pleater tape, 3⅞″ multi-pleater tape, iron-on pleater tape. Diagonal from top to bottom: transparent mini-pleater tape, lead weight tape, Austrian shade tape, zipper.

Pinch pleats or triple pleats are very traditional. The pleat is actually three small pleats grouped together at regular intervals. The beauty of pleater tape is that it has pockets woven into it that are evenly spaced.

By using four-pronged hooks inserted in the pockets, you'll get a perfect three-folded pleat. To determine the proper fullness, allow twice the track length.

Pencil pleats are the most popular. Pencil pleats create multiple folds in the curtain fabric. Hooks can be placed in one of three rows of pockets. For fullness, allow 2½ times the track length.

Cartridge pleats are used for curtains with a long drop. Cartridge pleater tape produces rows of cylindrical pleats. Allow two times the track length for fullness.

Box pleats are great for fixed position curtains and valances. Box pleat tape is 3″ wide to hide the track. The tape has two rows of hook pockets so you can use split hooks. Allow three times the track length for fullness.

The heading for **goblet pleats** is extra wide and forms deep shaped pleats. Allow two times the track length for fullness.

Smocked pleats create a smocked look great for valances and curtains. You can use standard hooks placed in one or two rows of the hook pockets. Allow 2½ times the track length for fullness.

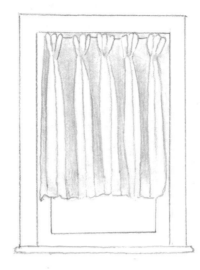

pinch pleats

pleater tape for pinch pleats

pinch pleats

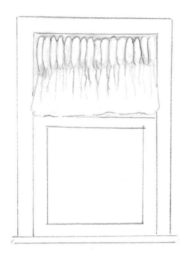

pencil pleats

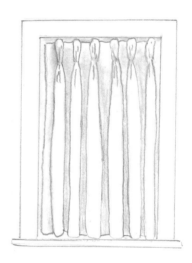

cartridge pleats

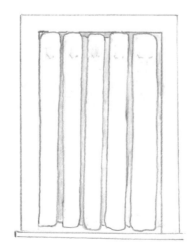

box pleats

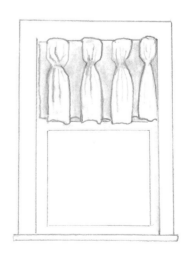

goblet pleats

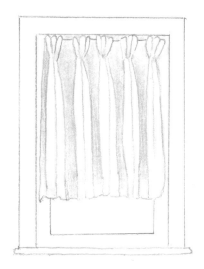

smocked pleats

There are also pleater tapes available for a simple gathered heading. This type is a narrow tape that helps form gathers on small-scale curtains. Allow 1½ to 2 times the track length for fullness.

For sheer or net fabrics, use sheer or net pleater tapes. This type of tape will form very thin pencil pleats. You can use standard hooks or slip a curtain rod through the loops in the tape. Allow twice the track length for fullness.

Applying the pleater tape doesn't have to be a chore. After the curtain is hemmed, measure up from the bottom to the desired length and fold down the fabric on this mark. Press in place. Cut the pleater tape the width of the curtain plus 1½". Place the tape below the top fold and turn

the ends of the tape under 3/4", lining up the side edge. Machine stitch along the ends of the tape, across the top and bottom edges of the tape. Sew in the same direction to eliminate puckers. Another method is to place the pleater tape at the top edge, with right sides together. Stitch across the top and turn the pleater tape to the wrong side of the curtain. Then stitch across the top and bottom of the tape and across the ends.

Tip

When setting pleats in curtains, use a damp cloth rinsed in white vinegar and water (50/50). The pleats will be set forever.

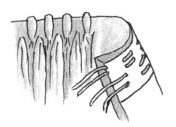

smocking tape

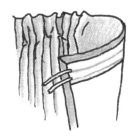

2-cord shirring tape

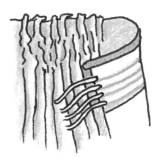

4-cord shirring tape

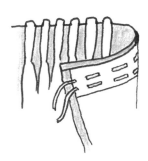

2-cord pencil pleat tape

DRAW CORD TAPES

Draw cord tapes are very simple to use and give you an even, finished look.

Smocking tape has cords that run through the tape - two at the top and two at the bottom of the tape. By drawing the cords, you create the look of a hand-smocked heading.

Shirring tape has either two or four cords that are evenly spaced so you can gather them in even rows.

Pencil pleat tape comes in two-cord or four-cord. The two-cord gives you a 1" deep pleat and the four-cord gives you a 4" deep pencil pleat.

FUSING INSTEAD OF SEWING

Not everyone wants to sew when taking on home decorating projects. Is it possible? Yes, it certainly is. There is indeed a way around the sewing machine.

One innovation that allows for no-sew curtains is fusible drapery tape. The backing on the drapery tape has an adhesive that sticks when heat and steam hit it. Using this you can achieve perfect pleats, smocking, faultless gathers, and more. This is also convenient to use on valances, dust ruffles, vanity skirts, and covered wastebaskets. You simply position the tape on the wrong side of the fabric and fuse. Then draw up the tape cords to the size you need for gathers or pleats. Some of these products attach with hook and loop

fasteners for mounting to most any surface (see page 137). Fusible shade products are also available. This rubber-backed interfacing can be used with fabric to create customized window shades.

Paper-backed webbing, called fusible bonding web, can be used to bond two pieces of fabric together. This is available in fabric widths as well as narrow widths for hems and applying trims.

Fusible fleece is a low loft batting product with an adhesive back. (Hard to believe, I know - a sheep that is fused to the side of a mountain!) This is ideal for adding dimension to items such as headboards, band boxes, and cornice boards. It is also great for padded picture frames, mirror

Getting ready to apply fusible fleece to a headboard.

frames, tissue box covers, and more. There are glues designed specifically for use with fabric and trimmings.

CASINGS

If you prefer to make a casing rather than use pleater tapes, do so. Place the curtain rod in the casing and either gather the fabric or leave it ungathered. The ungathered look is good for panels made of lace or

decorative fabrics. To add a bit of drama, fold open the curtain and tack it back. When gathering, allow one to 1½ times the width of the rod for fullness.

ungathered

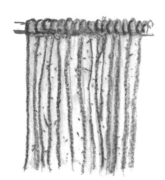

gathered

Fold back the ungathered panels and tack them for "Arabian" or "tent" flaps.

HEADINGS

To achieve a heading that extends above the casing, fold down a double hem that is deep enough to equal the top frill and width of the pocket. If you don't want that extension, fold down a double hem that equals the width of the pocket only.

Stitch close to the bottom fold of this hem. Measure up the width of the rod (plus a slight ease) and stitch again. This gives you the casing. Machine stitch in the same direction to avoid puckering.

Case Headings

This heading is quite simple and is often used for kitchen or bathroom curtains and for sheers that go behind a drape or in a small window above the main window. Make a casing at the top and bottom.

This valance features a simple casing with a 2″ heading. The extra fullness is achieved by allowing 2 to 2½ times the width.

This heading is cuffed and embellished with attached fringe. The sheer is on a separate single rod. These casual panels give the look of a folded over heading when in reality they are drapes (that droop).

This bordered sheer features a rod pocket on top and bottom.

SWAGS

Swags are an easy and quick way to treat a window. Suitable fabrics include small to medium scale prints and solids of cottons and cotton blends in light to medium weights. This will allow the fabric to fall softly into folds. When installing the hardware for swags, it is best to install it right on the window frame or 1″ to 2″ beyond the frame. Install the wood pole brackets or swag holders first so you can drape a tape measure across the brackets. Let the tape hang down in the middle to determine just how long the fabric needs to be. Allow the tape measure to hang down at the sides also. You will be able to get a finished length by doing this.

MAKING A SIMPLE THROW SWAG
(OR WINDOW SCARF)

Materials:

For unlined:
❈ Fabric (45″ or 54″ wide): the finished length desired plus 1″ for hems
❈ Brackets
❈ Thread to match

For lined:
❈ Fabric (45″ or 54″ wide) the finished length desired plus 1″ for hems
❈ Lining fabric (45″ or 54″ wide): an equal amount of a complementary fabric
❈ Brackets
❈ Thread to match

Instructions:

1. Cut the fabric the length you need. I have found the easiest way to do this is to drape a 120″ tape measure across the window. Allow for the side lengths and be sure to drape the center as low as you want it. Take that measurement and add 1″ for the hems.

2. Finish the raw edges of the fabric by turning the fabric under 1/4″ and stitching a narrow hem across the short ends. You can use the selvage edges of the fabric as a hem along the entire length. You can also roll hem this edge on your serger.

3. If lining, put right sides together and stitch the fabric to the lining 1/2″ from the edge all the way around. Leave a small opening so you can turn the fabric to the right side. Turn. Whipstitch the opening and press.

Hanging Directions:

1. Divide the finished material in half and place the center of the material in the center of the window when you put it over the rod.

2. Adjust the folds on the width of the window to create the look of a swag.

3. Use a thumb tack on the back of the wooden pole to secure the fabric. Adjust the tapers.

Another variation of the above: Use a longer piece of fabric and wrap the fabric around the pole twice. Swags can be many lengths - to the floor, to the bottom of a window, and of course, valance length.

TRADITIONAL SWAGS

A traditional swag usually has folds that come to a point on the sides and overlap the last fold. Doing this eliminates extra bulk across the top of the board. The fabric can be cut on the straight of the grain or on a bias cut. Various pattern companies have swag patterns in the home decorating section of their pattern books. I recommend you look one of these over to get an idea of how the pieces should look to acquire the folds, drape, and sides. They can be lined or unlined.

MAKING A SIMPLE
BALLOON VALANCE

A balloon shade is gathered only at the lower edge and I have tried for years to figure out why it is called a balloon. This particular balloon valance is stuffed with tissue paper to give the puffy look. You can make two poufs with each width of fabric. A longer balloon valance measures 21″ from the rod, while a shorter version hangs 18″.

Materials:

* Fabric (See step 1)
* Curtain rod of your choice
* Tissue paper
* Thread to match

Instructions:

1. Measure the rod and the returns. To find the cutting length, multiply the total rod and return measurement by 2½ and add 4″ for two 1″ double hems. The fabric width for the longer version is 43″ wide and 37″ for the shorter version. Cut each fabric width to the proper length (one fabric width for every two poufs).

2. Right sides together, sew the widths together.

3. On the sides, turn under 1/4″ on the raw edge and press. Turn another 3/4″ and stitch.

4. On the upper edge, turn under 1/2″ and press. Turn another 1½″ and press again.

5. On the lower edge, turn under 1/2″ and press. Fold the lower edge up and under the pressed edge of the upper turn. Carefully catch all thicknesses and stitch the entire width of the valance.

6. Place the valance on the rod, gathering the fabric on the rod for the balloon effect. Stuff with tissue paper to add the "poufs."

MAKING A ROMAN SHADE

Roman shades are so unique because when they are down, they are completely flat. When they are up, they don't roll, but they pleat in beautiful deep horizontal pleats. These shades give a tailored look to any room and are especially nice in an office. Because the material list is longer than most, it gives the impression that they are more difficult to make. Not so. This will be a great adventure. There are patterns for this particular shade that will help with cutting the fabric.

MAKING A TAB ROMAN SHADE

The instructions are the same as for the Roman Shade except instead of mounting the upper edge of the shade on the mounting board, sew tabs to the top edge. The tabs fit over a pole. Evenly space the tabs across the top, then stitch a matching fabric piece over the tabs and turn to the inside.

Materials:

❀ Decorator fabric: Refer to the chart below. You need a piece of fabric the width and length of the finished shade plus 3″.

❀ Lining fabric: Refer to the chart. Cut the lining width to equal the finished width and the length to equal the finished length plus 3″. Cut the facing strip from the lining fabric 5″ wide and the length equal to the finished length plus 3″.

❀ Thread to match

❀ Mounting board 1″ x 2″ cut to size for inside mounting. Paint the ends so they won't show

❀ Screw eyes: number equal to number of vertical rows

❀ Shade cord: long enough to go up the shade, across the top, and part way down the side

❀ Ring tape: length of shade multiplied by the number of vertical rows, plus 6″

❀ Weight rod: one 3/8″ brass rod or 1/2″ rustproof flat bar, cut 1/2″ shorter than the finished width of the shade

❀ White glue

❀ Awning cleat

❀ Staple gun

Window Length	Fabric Width	Window Width 26″ to 42″
30″ to 34″	45″	1¼ yds.
	54″	1¼ yds.
35″ to 40″	45″	1½ yds.
	54″	1½ yds.
41″ to 46″	45″	1⅝ yds.
	54″	1⅝ yds.
47″ to 52″	45″	1¾ yds.
	54″	1¾ yds.
53″ to 60″	45″	2 yds.
	54″	2 yds.

Instructions:

1. Place the decorator fabric wrong side up on the table. Using your seam gauge, mark the finished width. Fold the sides in 1½″ and press.

2. Place the lining on the decorator fabric, wrong sides together. Make sure the lining is under the side hems. Pin it in place so it won't shift.

3. On the right side of the shade fabric, center the facing strip on the lower edge and pin. The facing strip should extend 1″ beyond each side. Stitch 1/2″ from the lower edge. Press this strip to the wrong side of the shade fabric.

4. Press the 1″ extensions to the back of the shade. Stitch in place.

5. Turn the raw edge of the facing strip under 1½″ and 1½″ again. Stitch along this folded edge and again 1″ apart from it. This forms the pocket.

6. Place the ring tape in vertical rows. Be sure each row lines up horizontally. Turn under the tape edge that butts the top of the rod pocket. Use the zipper foot and stitch the tape down.

7. Staple the top edge of the fabric to the mounting board.

8. Where the ring tape meets the board, insert one screw eye.

9. Tie the cord in the right bottom ring and thread through this row of vertical rings. Do the same for the middle row of rings, taking the cord through the center screw eye and over to the first row, leaving extra for pulling. Thread the last row of rings, taking the cord through the remaining screw eye and over through the next screw eye and join up with the other cords.

10. Place the weight rod in the rod pocket.

11. Mount the shade to the wall.

12. With the shade down, adjust the cords so they allow the shade to lay perfectly flat. Tie the cords together, just below the screw eye.

13. Place the awning cleat on the wall. This is where you will tie the cords when you want to raise the shade.

For a stagecoach affect, cut strips of fabric that can be stapled to the mounting board and tied when the shade is up.

MAKING A CLOUD SHADE

A cornice board is not always necessary because of the gathered heading, but a mounting board can be used. These are called clouds because they give you the affect that something is "light and airy" sort of like puffy clouds. Sheer fabric would be ideal for this project.

Materials:

❁ Decorator fabric: 3 times the width and 12″ longer than the window
❁ Facing strip: 4″ wide and the length of the width of the fabric plus 1″
❁ Four-cord shirring tape: same length as the width of the shade
Mounting board
❁ 1″ rod
❁ Ring tape
❁ Screw eyes
❁ Shade cord
❁ Weight rod
❁ Awning cleat

Instructions:

1. Stitch a 1″ double-fold hem on the sides and lower edge.
2. On the upper edge, fold down 3¾″. Place the shirring tape 1/4″ down from the fold and pin. Using the zipper foot, stitch on each side of all four cords.
3. Place the ring tape as described in the Roman Shade directions on page 101.
4. On one side of the shirring tape, tie a knot in all four cords. On the other side, pull the cords to be the same width as the mounting board. Knot the cords.
5. On the facing strip, press under 1/2″ on short ends. Fold the strip in half lengthwise, wrong sides together.

6. On the right side of the shade, pin the raw edges of the strip right above the shirring tape and stitch 1/2″ from the edge.
7. Staple the facing strip to the top of the mounting board.
8. Tie together the bottom three rings of each vertical row. This will give you that puffy look.
9. To string, refer to the directions for the Roman Shade on page 101.
10. Cover the weight row with matching fabric and insert the rod in the lower hem. Gather the fabric evenly along the rod.

MAKING ROSETTES

Rosettes are a wonderful way to add a special touch to swags, tiebacks, or valances. A rosette is actually a gathered strip of fabric that is rolled up tightly and secured. They work better when you use a crisp fabric such as moiré or chintz or polished cotton.

Materials:

To make one 7" rosette
* Strip of fabric 7″ wide and 72″ long
* Needle and thread

Instructions:

1. Fold the fabric strip in half lengthwise with wrong sides together. Serge the edge together, including the short ends. Press.

2. Using a basting stitch, stitch along the long edge 1/2″ down from the edge. Gather tightly.

3. Starting at one end, roll the strip tightly for a few turns. This will be the center of the rosette.

4. Continue rolling loosely toward the other end, tacking as you go.

5. When you reach the opposite end, secure the ends and fluff up the rose by spreading the petals.

6. Hand tack the rosette in place.

PATTERN REPEAT IN CURTAINS

Some fabrics have a picture or design that repeats itself over and over again. Locate a complete picture or motif and measure it from top to bottom. In the photo, notice the distance from the larger white shell to the matching shell. This is a good example of pattern repeat.

Allow a single pattern repeat for each drop of the curtain. This will allow you to match the pattern across seams from one curtain to another.

All patterns have a repeat, but in some it's not noticeable. On this shell pattern, you can really see the repeat and need to allow for it when buying fabric and planning the design.

LINING

To line or not to line? That is the question.

Unlined Curtains

❧ Are easy to make, so are a good beginner curtain project.
❧ Are easier to wash, so are a good choice for windows in high traffic areas.
❧ Allow more light to come through.

Lined Curtains

❧ Have more body so the curtain will hang well.
❧ Keep out light.
❧ Add privacy.
❧ If you use interlining, lined curtains will help insulate your window from the heat and cold.

Above: This unlined window treatment features a cotton damask stripe with a gauze header and moss fringe. The sides are pulled up over finials.
Left: Two large and one small swag with cascades in two lengths made from heavy lined linen fabric. The shorter cascades are made from fabric lined with a contrasting color.

MAKING LINED CURTAINS

If you choose to line your curtains, select a lining fabric equal in weight to the curtain fabric. Sateen is often used as lining material. Be sure to install the curtain rod before measuring for yardage requirements.

Materials:

❋ Decorator fabric: Refer to Chapter Six. Include a 4″ double-fold hem.
❋ Lining fabric: Cut the lining fabric 6″ narrower than the decorator fabric and 5½″ shorter than the finished curtain.
❋ Thread to match
❋ Weights: 1 for each inside corner of the bottom hem allowance

Instructions:

1. Press and stitch a 4″ double-fold hem in the curtain fabric.
2. Press and stitch a 2″ double-fold hem in the lining fabric.
3. Place the lining and curtain fabrics right sides together. Make sure the lining hem is 1½″ above the curtain hem. Pin and stitch 1/2″ seams on sides.

4. Place the curtain decorator fabric side down. Make sure you have an equal amount of curtain fabric turned back over each side of the lining. Press the side seams toward the lining.
5. Turn the curtain to the right side. Check to see if the side hems are of equal width.

6. Align the upper edge of the lining with the finished length marking on the curtain. Press the side hems. At the unfinished upper edges, press under an amount equal to the side hems.
7. Turn the upper edge of the curtain down along the lining to form a casing and/or heading. Stitch the casing.

8. Hand tack weights along the lower edge of the curtain inside the side hems and the seams.

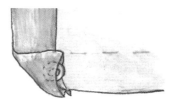

9. Turn the side hem back diagonally below the lining. This is a form of mitering. Slipstitch or whipstitch. Press.

10. Insert the curtain rod in the casing and hang.

MAKING PINCH PLEATED
UNLINED DRAPERIES

Nothing makes this easier than store bought pleater tape. The tape contains little pockets for the hooks and automatically creates perfect pleats. These hooks can be removed to wash the drapes, which is also convenient. Be sure to install the curtain rod before measuring.

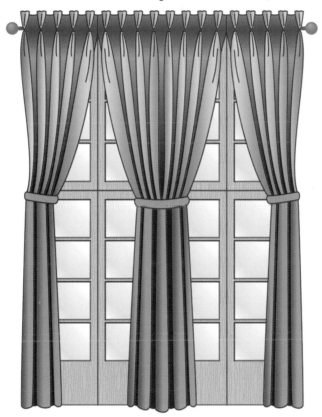

Materials:

❋ Fabric: Refer Chapter Six. The formula below will give you a rough idea.

      Rod width
      + 2 returns
      + overlap
      = pair widths

❋ Pinch pleater tape
❋ Drapery hooks: two-pronged or three-pronged
❋ Thread to match

Instructions:

1. When cutting the fabric, keep in mind that the final width should be 2½ times the width of the window. The length is yours to determine. If the fabric isn't wide enough, you will have to cut lengths of fabric and sew them together, right sides together.

2. Start with the sides and turn under the edge 1″ and fold over again. Stitch.

3. Fold the top edge over 2″ wider than the pleater tape. Turn the raw edge under 1″ and press. Stitch next to this fold.

4. Place the pleater tape 1/2″ down from the top edge on the wrong side. Pin. Stitch the pleater tape in place close to the edges of the pleater tape. Use this edge as a guideline.

5. You can turn up and stitch the bottom edge of the drape now or wait until you hang the drape and pin the hem in place. This depends on how sure you are about the length of the curtain.

6. Insert a hook at each end and one in the middle. Work from the middle to each side. Two-pronged hooks use less fabric than three-pronged hooks. How full you want the curtain will determine which one to use. Each pleat needs to be the same.

7. Hang the curtain/drape.

MAKING A CORNICE BOARD

Customizing your own cornice board makes it possible for you to coordinate the cornice with your drapery fabric or other special touches in the room. The challenge of making a cornice board can be quite rewarding. Even if you have never picked up a hammer, you can build this cornice board. It's a good idea to make the sides at least 6″ deep, so the cornice board protrudes from the wall 6″.

Materials:

* 1/2″ plywood cut in the size and shape desired (front piece, top piece, and two side pieces)
* Decorator fabric: 10″ longer than the total dimension of the three sides of cornice board and 10″ longer than the widest point from top to bottom
* Batting to pad board, 1/2″ thick
* Brackets and screws
* Carpenter's glue
* Finishing nails

Instructions:

1. Measure the area where the cornice board will be mounted. The cornice should clear 3″ above the heading and extend 2″ beyond the end of the drapery at each side. These are the inside measurements of the cornice board. The front and top piece of wood should be the same.

2. Cut the sides the same as the height of the cornice and the depth of the top of the cornice. Don't forget to add for the thickness of the plywood.

3. Assemble the boards using finishing nails.

Covering the Board:

1. Place the board face down on the batting and trace. Cut the batting out and staple it to the board.

2. Lay the padded cornice board face down on the fabric and trace. Add 3″ around all the traced lines so you will have enough to wrap and tuck. Cut the fabric out using the outer line

3. Pull the fabric taut and staple the fabric to the back of the cornice board, starting in the front middle. Work from the middle to the outer edges. Pull and staple and clip when necessary. You will need to clip around curved edges. Be careful not to clip too far into the fabric.

4. Nail brackets to each end of the cornice board and attach it to the wall.

MAKING A TAPERED VALANCE

When a tapered valance is hung on a rod, it looks like one piece of fabric that has been cut longer on each side. Actually it is six pieces of fabric (three front, three lining). Many patterns can be found for this type of valance. Once you see the shape of the pieces involved, the rest is simple.

Materials:

To make a valance for a 35″ to 44″ wide window

❀ Decorator fabric: 2¼ yds. of 45″ wide or 1¾ yds. of 54″ wide
❀ Lining: same as decorator fabric
❀ 1" width rod
❀ Thread to match

Instructions:

1. Cut the center piece 21½″ long x 14″ wide. Place the length on the fold. This will give you one long piece that is 43″ long x 14″ wide. The tapered pieces are shaped as shown.

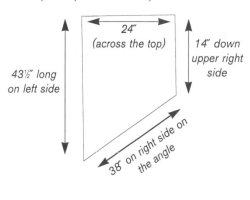

2. With right sides together, stitch the three lining pieces together as shown. Repeat for the three front pieces.

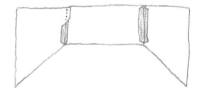

3. With right sides together, sew the front and the lining together, sewing a row of stitches 2″ from the edge. Leave an opening for turning.

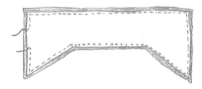

4. Turn right side out and stitch the opening.

5. Stitch again 1½″ down from the first row of stitches on the top edge to form the casing.

6. To open the casing on the sides, simply remove the stitches between the rod pocket stitching. Insert the rod.

MAKING A SOFT VALANCE

This can be used as the basis for many cornices. You can add triangles as I did, or any other trims. The possibilities are endless.

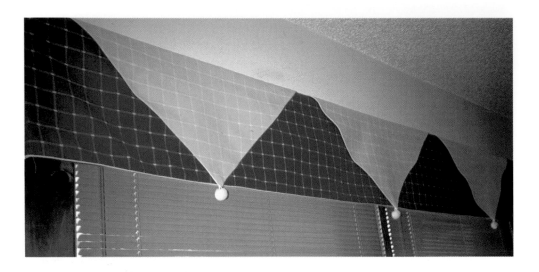

Materials:

❦ Decorator fabric: For a 37″ or 43″ window: 1 yd. of 45″ wide or 3/4 yd. of 54″ wide. For a 52″ window: 1½ yds. of 45″ wide or 1 yd. of 54″ wide
Lining fabric: same as decorator fabric
❦ Contrasting fabric for triangles: 1 yd. of 45″ or wider
❦ Piping, 2½ yds.
❦ Thread to match

Instructions:

1. Measure the width of the window and decide how deep you want the valance to be. Calculate yardage for the long stretch of valance (the blue part in the photo). Then calculate

yardage for the accent triangles using the suggestions above.
2. Cut the fabric and lining the width of the window plus 2″ on each side for hems. Cut it the length plus 5/8″ for the bottom hem plus 1″ for applying it to the cornice board on top.
3. Cut yellow piping the same length as the blue valance.
4. Use the zipper foot to sew the yellow piping to the two short sides and one long side.

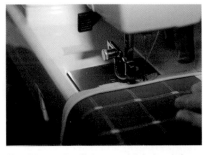

5. Place the lining and fabric, right sides together, and stitch the ends and one long side.
6. Clip the seams, turn right side out. Press. Turn the ends in again 1″, secure and press.

7. This window is wide enough to break up the width with three yellow triangles. To make the three yellow triangles, cut six triangles of fabric the size you want and six triangles from lining.
8. With right sides together, stitch the fabric and lining pieces together with a fringe ball at the point of each triangle, leaving an opening across the top for turning.
9. Clip the seams, turn right side out, and press.
10. Mark placement on the length of the blue valance to insure that the three triangles will be evenly spaced. Stitch the triangles to the valance using a basic machine stitch.
11. Staple the valance to the cornice board.
12. Rest the board on top of the window molding to find the exact placement for the angle brackets. Secure the brackets to the underside of the board, then attach the board to the wall.

MAKING A BOX PLEATED VALANCE

Another variation is the box pleated valance. This gives a more formal look. The inverted box pleat is most common with a straight edge but can also be made with a scalloped edge.

The box pleated valances in this room add a touch of elegance and a finished look to the window treatment.

Materials:

❁ Fabric: twice as much as the finished length of the valance. For example: for a 6 foot finished valance, you will need 12 feet (4 yds.) of fabric. If the pattern has to be matched, buy extra fabric.
❁ Thread to match
❁ Velcro

Instructions:

1. Cut strips of fabric that are 16″ wide and twice the length needed.
2. Turn under the long raw edge 1/4″ and stitch or press down.
3. Pleats are usually 2″ deep and 5″ apart. Working on the right side of the fabric, start at one edge and measure 5″ in. Then measure 4″, another 5″, and another 4″ until you reach the end. Bring the 4″ measurements together making a 2″ pleat. Pin.

4. Press the pleats flat after stitching along the top to secure the pleats.
5. Cut a strip of Velcro the length of the valance. Sew it close to the top of the valance. Attach the opposing piece of Velcro to the wooden frame. Press the Velcro together and you have a box pleated valance.

TIEBACKS

While going from house to house with the photographer and interior decorator, I was intrigued by all the fancy curtain tiebacks. I saw everything from fun to dramatic, to inconspicuous, to braided, to shaped and more. There were even ruffled tiebacks, big bows, banded, contour, shirred rope, and just plain straight. The one I loved the most was the braided tieback. Most tiebacks are 18″ to 44″ long. To determine the length tieback you need, pretend your tape measure is a tieback or use the chart below. The more panels there are in your draperies or curtains, the longer tieback you'll need to hold it. As it gets bulkier, the tie needs to be longer.

Use the fabric from the curtain or fabric that is compatible with your curtain. Various colors or one color - the choice is yours.

Panel Size	Tieback Length
1 width	22″
2 widths	28″
3 widths	36″
4 widths	44″

Example of a straight tieback with trim

A plain straight tieback

Instructions:

1. Cut a strip the length you need and double the width you need, plus 1″.

2. Fold right sides together lengthwise and sew 1/2″ from the raw edges, starting at one end adn sewing toward the middle. Break the stitch and continue to the other end. The small opening is for turning.

3. Clip the corners, turn, and press.

4. Slipstitch the opening closed.

5. Choose a closure type (Velcro, snaps, buttons, hook and eye) and sew them on.

MAKING A BRAIDED TIEBACK

Materials:

❈ Fabric: 1 yd. (if using two colors, 1/2 yd. of each)
❈ Batting
❈ Thread to match

Instructions:

1. Cut six strips of fabric 3½" wide and twice the length of the finished tieback (six all one color or three strips of two colors or two strips of three colors).

2. Cut six strips of batting 3" wide and twice the length of the finished tieback.

3. Fold the fabric strips right sides together with the batting strip inside and stitch each with a 1/2" seam lengthwise. Move the seam so it is centered on the batting strip. This will keep it from being seen.

4. Hand stitch three strips together at the top and start braiding. Right over left. Left over right. Right over left and so on.

5. When you finish braiding, stitch the ends together. Fold a 3" square of fabric over the ends to hide the tails.

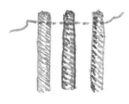

MAKING TASSELS

Another idea I saw was the use of tassels with tiebacks. Tassels also work well with envelope pillows, table-cloths, or shade pulls. Tassels add a splash of color and a dash of character. Using tassels will definitely give you fringe benefits!

Materials:

To make a 6″ tassel:
* 6 oz. of 4-ply yarn
* 8″ x 12″ piece of cardboard

Instructions:

1. Buy enough yarn to make the number of tassels you want. Figure approximately six ounces of yarn per tassel.

2. Cut a piece of cardboard 8″ wide x 12″ long. For longer or shorter tassels, adjust the length of the cardboard. This size cardboard will make a tassel 6″ long.

3. With the cut end at the bottom edge, wrap the yarn lengthwise around the cardboard 25 to 30 times.

4. Slip a 6″ piece of strong thread under the yarn at the top of the cardboard and tie the ends of the thread securely to pull the yarn together. Use a longer piece of thread to bind the tassel top if you plan to fasten the tassel to a pillow.

5. Braid 12 strands of yarn 10″ to 12″ long to make a 6″ braid for the tassel top. Form the braid into a circle and knot the ends. Slip the circle under the yarn at the top edge of the cardboard. Take one side of the circle over the yarn and thread through the opposite side of the circle. Pull to form a loop.

6. Cut the yarn along the bottom edge of the cardboard.

7. To form the tassel head, wrap a piece of yarn around all the strands about 1/4 the way down from the loop. Leave one end of the yarn free before you wrap and tie this securely to the other end of the yarn after you finish wrapping.

8. Shake out the tassel to free all the strands. Trim the bottom edges even.

HELPFUL INNOVATIONS IN THE DRAPERY DEPARTMENT

There are many new and not so new items in the drapery department that make creating window treatments much easier than it was years ago. The list is long but it certainly is worth knowing these items exist.

❀ Temporary window shades - one size fits all. These are great for someone who has moved into a new house and doesn't have the drapes up yet. When in place, you simply cut the shade to size.

❀ Curtain rods for steel doors. You might have a window in an office door, back door, or even a van door. It is almost impossible to drill into steel, so these rods can be put in place and a window treatment added with no extra drilling.

❀ Kits to make a roll-up window shade. All you add is the fabric.

❀ Decorator pole sets/decorative rings and finials.

❀ Tack strips 27″ long. These are used in upholstery jobs. This strip is tacked under the front edge of a chair or couch and the fabric is attached to the strip. Most chairs are 27″ wide. If not, the strips can be tacked next to each other.

❀ Drapery hooks with two and three prong hooks. Use two prong for lighter fabrics and three prong for heavier fabrics.

❀ Clip-on hooks. Used often in café curtains. No need to sew these, just clip them on.

❀ Drapery weights encased in white fabric. These are added to the hem of drapes to make them hang properly. Having them already encased means you won't have to make a sleeve for them.

❀ Kits to convert a standard rod to 2½″ deep by adding a wide backing.

❀ Hardware to create window treatments for odd-shaped windows such as oval, sunburst, octagonal, and porthole. The hardware just clips onto these odd-shaped windows.

❀ Cornice extender kits. You can extend a cornice up to 77″. This may be necessary for a sliding glass door. No sewing involved.

❀ Adjustable cornice kits with or without fabric sleeves. These cornice kits are used primarily over vertical blinds. You slip the fabric over the cornice and have an instant finished cornice board.

❀ Dauphine rods 2½″ to 4½″. If you use the 2½″ rod you can have two window treatments at the same time. The 4½″ rod is only for one window treatment.

❀ Curtain jewelry. Some of these are magnetic and are used for tiebacks. The jewelry is in front and the magnetic piece is hidden behind the curtain. No sewing necessary.

❀ Swag rings. These are wooden or metal rings on a pole.

❀ Sconces. These are mounted to the wall on each side of the window. They have a hole in the middle and you can either place a pole in each hole or just drape fabric through them.

❀ Clip-on drapery rings to match the rod, much like the rings used in café curtains. It is nice to know you can match the rod so they won't show as much.

Even though curtains are used primarily for privacy, warmth, and keeping out noise, we all get great pleasure from looking at gorgeous window treatments. It's just one more way of making your house a beautiful home.

Curtains fill spaces.

CHAPTER THIRTEEN

The Bedroom – A Private Place at Any Age

Your bedroom is your place to go and hide. I consider the bedroom a very private area, but at times it does include children and pets running through. In the early Middle Ages, one of the rooms that developed off the drawing room was the sleeping chamber. People usually slept on the floor or on mattresses laid on cords stretched on a wooden frame. During the 16th century, the bedroom was used as a family living room. During the Renaissance and 17th century, the bedroom was richly furnished. Thankfully, during the 18th century the bedroom took on a less pretentious look.

Bedroom suites were popular back then and can be reproduced in today's home if you have the room, but most people opt for a very large bathroom rather than a sitting room. An accurate definition of a bedroom is a room for your bed. This is a room for intimacy, sleep, and changing clothes. The bedroom has a door that can be kept closed if it doesn't match the rest of the house or isn't as neat as you'd like it - a solution when all else fails. The closed door also comes in handy when adults (or children) need a place to go and scream.

When you decorate a bedroom, the first consideration should be whose bedroom it is. Whoever is going to live there needs to be consulted when choosing fabrics, colors, and perhaps a theme. Children can take great pride in their room if extended the courtesy of being asked what they like and what they don't.

Obviously, the bed takes up the largest space in the room and can't help but be the centerpiece. A bed can become a family hangout, a place for reading, a place to talk on the phone, a place for inspiration, and of course, a place to sleep. Decorating your bedroom is a perfect way to combine lifestyle with personal style.

These days, we have more ways to cover the bed than just bedspreads. We can choose from comforters, duvet covers, quilts, and even add a bed ruffle.

MAKING A THROW BEDSPREAD

A bedspread truly "covers the bed." The spread extends to the floor and there is enough added length to allow for tucking under and wrapping the pillows. Have fun with this - it is a simple and fast way to change an entire bedroom.

Materials:

❋ Fabric (54″ wide): twin or full bed 7½ yds.; queen or king bed 11¼ yds.
❋ Trim (such as cording): measure the length of the bed + 18″ for tuck x 2, then add the width. The yardage will be somewhere between 5 to 7 yds. (placed in seams where the sides are attached)
❋ Thread to match

Instructions:

1. When piecing the fabric, avoid a center seam. Create a wide center section and two narrower side sections.

For a twin bed, make the center section 40″ wide plus 1″ for seams. After you subtract 40″ from the total width, divide the difference into two equal width side sections.

For a double, queen, or king size bed, use the full width of the fabric minus 1″ for seams. Subtract the center section from the total width, divide the difference into two equal width side sections. Add 2½″ to the side sections for hem allowance.

2. If using piping, cording, or other trims, sew it on the entire length of each side of the center sections before sewing the three sections together.

3. Right sides together, sew the three sections together, using 1/2″ seam allowances.

4. Hem the side sections first and then the top and bottom.

Tip

The amount of cording needed for a twin or full size bed is 9½ yds. (for the outside edge). For a queen or king size bed, you'll need 10½ yds. (for the outside edge).

MAKING A BASIC DUVET COVER

A comforter or coverlet is like a bedspread but shorter. A comforter only extends 4″ or 5″ below the mattress so it is usually accompanied by a bed ruffle and shams because a comforter isn't long enough to hide the pillows.

These two comforters illustrate how dramatically fabric influences decor.

A duvet cover is like an oversize pillowcase. This cover goes over a down-filled blanket (duvet) that provides warmth without weight. A duvet generally looks like a white comforter.

Materials:

* Fabric (54″ wide): twin and full size 7¾ yds.; queen and king size 11 yds.
* Thread
* Zipper, buttons, or Velcro

Instructions:

1. When piecing, avoid a center seam. Try to piece the fabric so you end up with one center section and two equal side sections.

2. Cut and piece the top and bottom of the duvet cover, adding a 1/2″ seam allowance. On the bottom piece add 2″ to the length.

3. On the bottom piece, measure up 8″ and cut off. Make a seam by sewing it back together and add a zipper in this seam. (This is the easiest way to do it.)

4. If adding trim/cording/piping, add it now to the top piece.

5. With the zipper open, place the top and bottom piece right sides together. Use a 1/2″ seam allowance and stitch all the way around the duvet cover.

6. Turn the cover right side out.

Tip

If using cord on all four sides of a duvet cover, you will need 8¾ yds. for a twin bed, 9 yds. for a full, 10 yds. for a queen, and 11 yds. for a king.

MAKING A GATHERED BED RUFFLE

Whether you call it a dust ruffle, bed ruffle, or bed skirt, this adds a nice finishing touch to bed coverings that don't reach the floor, such as comforters and duvets. The skirt hides the bottom half of the bed - the box spring, bed frame, and underbed storage space.

The bed ruffle is attached to a fabric "deck" that fits between the mattress and the box spring. I recommend using a fitted sheet as the deck when making a bed skirt. Just place the sheet over the box spring and trace around the top edge with a piece of chalk. Then attach the bed skirt or ruffle to the sheet along the marked line. A bed ruffle is usually open at the corners so it can get around bed legs or posts.

Materials:

❀ Fabric (48″ or wider): twin 7¼ yds.; full 8¼ yds.; queen 8¼ yds.; king 9 yds. (This will give you fullness 2½ times the width and length.)
❀ Bed sheet for the deck
❀ Thread to match

Instructions:

1. Using 1/2″ seam allowances, cut and piece the fabric to make two side skirt pieces and one end piece for the foot of the bed. (2½ times the measured length).

2. Hem the bottom edges and ends of all three pieces with 1″ double hems.

3. Gather the top edge of each piece using the serger or sewing machine.

4. You should now have three gathered lengths of fabric, two for the sides and one for the foot of the bed. With right sides together, begin pinning one of the side pieces to the deck; pinning from the head of the bed to the foot of the bed. As you are pinning, distribute the gathers evenly from the starting point to the corner. Pin until you reach the corner, then stitch the side piece to the deck with a 1/2″ seam allowance.

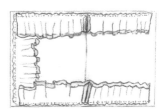

5. Pin the end piece to the deck, distributing the gathers evenly, and stitch with a 1/2″ seam allowance. Repeat with the last side piece. Remember to distribute the gathers evenly on all three sides so the finished skirt looks the same from either side.

6. Press the seam toward the deck, turn right side out, and topstitch.

MAKING A TAILORED BED SKIRT

Tailored bed skirts are ungathered and have inverted pleats at the corners. This is based on two tailored corners at the foot of the bed.

Materials:

* Fabric (48″ or wider): twin, full, or queen 6 yds.; king 6¾ yds.
* Bed sheet for the deck
* Thread to match

Instructions:

1. After cutting the correct number of lengths, stitch them together with a 1/2″ seam allowance at the short ends to make one long strip of fabric (long enough to encircle three sides of the bed and allow 40″ for the two inverted pleated corners).

2. Hem the bottom edge and ends with a 1″ double hem.

3. Right sides together, begin pinning the skirt to the deck at the head of the bed. Pin along one side until you reach the corner.

4. Fold and pin the fabric into an inverted pleat at the corner as shown.

5. Continue pinning to the other corner and repeat the inverted pleat. Continue pinning to the head of the bed on the opposite side of the starting point.

6. Stitch the skirt to the deck.

7. Press the seam toward the deck, turn right side out, and topstitch.

MAKING A BED CAP

In addition to the usual bedspread, comforter, or duvet cover, you may have the need for a bed cap. Bed caps are perfect for bunk beds. This type of bed is often used in a spare bedroom so the room will look like a den. A bed cap is like a coverlet with elastic around the outer edges so it will just snap onto the mattress. The size will vary according to the special beds. I thought it would be fun to add this to the book since you rarely see it explained in home decorating books.

A bed cap is ideal for bunk beds or beds that do double duty as a sofa.

Materials:

❋ Fabric: Refer to Chapter Six for yardage calculation instructions.
❋ Thread to match

Instructions:

1. Refer to making a bedspread for cutting and piecing the fabric.
2. To make the elastic corners, bring the right sides together on the diagonal.

3. Make a perpendicular line from the raw edge to the diagonal fold at the point equal to the measurement of the mattress drop plus 1˝.

4. Pin the two layers together and stitch along this line. Trim and turn.
5. Press under 1/2˝ along the entire outer edge, turn the edge up again 1/2˝ and stitch.

6. Add elastic at each corner by machine or by slipstitching it into the 1/2˝ hem.

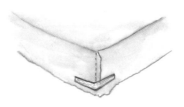

7. Turn up the hem and the elastic will be covered. The elastic will pull in the corner and it will be more likely to stay put when anyone decides to sit (or bounce) on the bed.

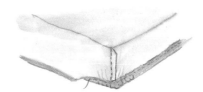

THE BABY'S ROOM

Nothing is more fun and rewarding than a home decorating project for the baby's room. This is one room that will give you a sense of accomplishment along with warm and fuzzy thoughts. Whether for your child or grandchild, this is what sewing is all about. This is the ultimate home decorating project.

A dust ruffle or skirt for a crib is made the same way as a gathered bed skirt (see page 119 for instructions) - just a simpler and smaller version. The ruffle actually sits on the wooden platform that lies below the mattress. The skirt length is up to you but the trend seems to be to the bottom of the sidebars when they are lowered.

Bumper guards keep the baby safe and secure. Naturally you can add lace, ruffles, or trims to these bumpers. That's where your personal creativity comes into play.

This crib features a matching dust ruffle, bumper guards, and canopy ruffle. Everything in this lovely nursery shows the love and care put into it.

MAKING BUMPER GUARDS

Materials:

* Fabric: 4⅜ yds. of 45″ wide
* Batting (2 layers): 4 yds. of 60″ wide
* Fusible interfacing: 1 yd.
* Thread to match
* Ribbon: 17½ yds. 1½″ wide for ties (or make your own from fabric)
Velcro

Cutting:
Fabric
* For the side bumpers, add 1″ to the length and depth of the mattress side and cut four.
* For the foot and head bumpers, add 1″ to the width and depth of the mattress and cut four.
* For the side flaps (this is what goes under the mattress to hold the bumper guards in place), add 1″ to the length and twice the depth of the mattress and cut four.
* For the headboard covering, make a pattern by tracing the shape of the headboard on a large piece of paper. Add 1″ on all edges and cut two.

Polyester batting
* Cut two side bumpers, one foot bumper, one head bumper.

Fusible interfacing
* Cut two side flaps.

Instructions:

1. If using purchased ribbon for the ties, cut 26 pieces 24″ long. If making fabric ties, cut 26 ties 1½″ wide x 24″ long. Fold them in half lengthwise, right sides together, and stitch along the long edge using a 1/4″ seam allowance. Turn right side out and press.

2. Baste the batting to the wrong side of each bumper piece.

3. Divide the upper edges of the side bumpers into fourths and mark. Fold each tie in half and pin them on these marks.

4. Fuse the interfacing to the wrong side of two flaps. Fold the flap in half lengthwise and stitch on the long edge. Turn and press. Pin the flap to the bottom edge of each side bumper.

5. Right sides together, pin the other bumper piece to the batted bumper. Stitch all four edges, leaving a small opening to turn to the right side. Trim the corners.

6. Slipstitch the opening closed. Do both side bumpers.

7. For the bumper at the foot of the crib, fold in half and mark. Add ties and continue as stated for the side bumpers (eliminating the flaps).

8. Repeat for the head bumper (also eliminating the flaps).

Another example of a perfectly coordinated nursery.

Popular themes for baby's rooms include cherubs, nursery rhymes, rabbits, teddy bears, and other baby animals. Don't forget the rocking chair - mother and baby user friendly.

Safety Tip

While photographing a nursery, I placed a small trinket on a shelf and the shelf fell down into the crib. Fortunately the baby wasn't there but it gave me a scare. Check items like that in your baby's room and don't forget to check the window treatment cords that are often right next to the crib - they can cause strangulation.

CHILDREN'S BEDROOMS

Decorating your child's room can be very rewarding. What makes it even more rewarding is including your child/children in the decision-making process. Ask if they would like a theme. What are their favorite colors? We all know the ultimate goal is teamwork, but there are some ways to steer your little decorator in the right direction. Asking him or her to keep the door closed is one solution to non-decorating but when the child takes part in the decorating process, they will want to show off their room. They will show pride in the finished product and may even keep the bed made.

A Matelasse' bedspread with a chintz bed ruffle and a printed chintz wicker love seat. Here is a room I would have wished for when growing up. This bedroom is a place where a little girl can dream and scheme (and her doll can dream along with her). The doll bed has a cotton cover with a ruffle and pink ribbon. Everything in this room coordinates and makes for an appealing little girl's bedroom and play area.

This Western room is "all boy." Everything from the lodge pole pine hand-crafted bed from Wyoming to the lodge pole pine chair with an elk skin bench makes a happy haven for any young man.

Obviously, fabric choices should be durable and easy-care. Keep in mind that children grow fast so don't choose something that has to be set in stone. Making throw pillows can give a special touch in a hurry and framing some of your child's favorite pictures makes it very personal. A growth chart for your child adds a nice touch. This is just another wonderful project for you and your child to plan together.

Tips for Decorating a Child's Room

❋ Don't assume your child was born to decorate. They will need some gentle guidance.

❋ Valances are easy to make and easy to change as tastes change.

❋ Don't assume your child wants what you want.

❋ Shop together for the toy chest - a place to clean up the clutter.

❋ Shop together for fabrics for the bedspread, pillows, and other small accessories.

❋ Build or buy bookshelves to display your child's favorite keep-sakes.

❋ Make a special spot for the family pet in your child's room.

The handmade quilt, ruffled shams, and coordinating headboard make this bed a comfortable spot for a favorite teddy bear.

The pillows and the valance really add appeal and color to this teen's bedroom. The teenager designed this herself with her mother's final okay. She created a soft cornice with banners. (Refer to Chapter Twelve for how to make a banner valance). The Marilyn Monroe theme was carried out by using blue, black, and pink on the envelope pillows. As the child grows older, continue stressing the fun in decorating. Look for prints that have cars, planes, trucks, rabbits, cats, or whatever they love the most. Use lots of happy colors - bold and beautiful. You can always accomplish a quick change by adding new pillows. Perhaps your children will grow up and want to create their own beautiful home. What a wonderful legacy!

Notice the adorable mix of patterns - stripes, dots, checks. Two colors carry the threme throughout the ruffle, bedspread, and pillows. Different size patterns can work together. Children love to mix and match.

MAKING A FABRIC WALL HANGING

It's fun to use fabrics with a distinctive print to make a wall hanging. Add a simple dowel and you have a colorful addition to your room.

Materials:

❀ Fabric with a design: yardage depends on size of wall hanging. For the one shown, I used 1 yd.
❀ Lining fabric: same as main fabric
❀ Cotton batting
❀ Dowel
❀ Thread to match

Instructions:

1. Cut a piece of the design fabric and lining fabric the width and length of your wall hanging. The one shown is 36″ square.

2. Stitch batting to the back of the fabric picture.

3. With right sides together, stitch the lining to the front piece, leaving a small opening to turn. Trim the seams and turn.

4. Use a slipstitch or whipstitch to close the opening.

5. Safety pin the three layers together to keep them from moving while you stitch around the design elements in the design. Stitch to your heart's content, the more the better, to give a three-dimensional effect.

6. Fold over the top edge and stitch it down to make the casing for the dowel.

7. Add the dowel and you are ready to hang it on the wall.

MAKING A TUFFET

Start with a simple stool and add a bit of foam, fabric, and trim, and you have a darling footstool.

Materials:

* Decorator fabric (54″ or wider): 1½ yds.
* Muslin (54″): 3/4 yd.
* Cord: 2 yds.
* Foam: piece the size of the stool seat, 1″ to 2″ thick
* Staple gun
* Thread to match

Instructions:

1. Cut a piece of foam to fit the top of the stool.
2. Stretch muslin over the foam and staple it to the underside of the stool.
3. Measure the stool from the floor, across the top, and back to the floor in both directions.
4. Cut a piece of fabric this size plus 1½" for the hem.
5. Turn under the hem 1/4″ twice and stitch.
6. Tie the cord around the stool. Tack in place.

BRIGHT IDEAS FOR THE BEDROOM

Sitting Area

It is very popular for a bedroom to include a sitting area. This usually includes a media center, small sofa and chair, and perhaps a small desk. What better place to curl up and read a good book? Choosing the curtains or valance over the sofa gives you an opportunity to personalize the area and match your bedroom.

Here the same fabric was used for the bed ruffle, tablecloth, and pillow shams. It really ties the look together.

BRIGHT IDEAS FOR THE BEDROOM

Notice how the bedroom flows from the bed to the sitting area.

Extra Storage Made Easy

How about box pleats that make pockets to hold anything from shoes to baby bottles? Make a row of box pleats (as long as you want) and sew them to a heavy piece of fabric. Add a dowel and hang it on the back of your closet door.

Decorating the bedroom can become a family affair. I met a husband and wife who took on the challenge of making a headboard. He cut the wood and she laid out the fabric and pressed it. He used the staple gun and she helped shape the fabric. The end result was a meaningful headboard for their granddaughter's bed. Or you can tackle the job yourself. How about making a padded seat for a chest to put at the foot of your bed?

The bedroom is the room that will be the most personal one you decorate. Take it in stride and you will once again add another notch in your "sew-a-beautiful-home" belt.

Beds, pillows, and people fill spaces.

CHAPTER FOURTEEN

The Bathroom - Take Some Time Out

A BATHROOM IS A PLACE WHERE YOU CAN GO TO ESCAPE, EVEN IF JUST FOR A SHORT TIME. A BATHROOM IS WHERE SOME PEOPLE SING IN THE SHOWER AND PRETEND THEY ARE THE NEXT FRANK SINATRA. IT'S A ROOM THAT ALLOWS YOU TO BE YOURSELF. WHEN STRESS TAKES ITS TOIL, RUN THE WATER, FLUSH THE TOILET, AND SCREAM. IT WILL HELP. A BATHROOM IS SMALL, COMPACT, AND FUN TO DECORATE.

MAKING A SHOWER CURTAIN

Shower curtains are an easy way to change the look of a bathroom. Choosing various holiday prints, you can change the bathroom with each holiday. This is particularly fun for children.

When making your own shower curtain, consider making it longer than the regular store bought curtain. An additional 8" gives added coverage and keeps water off the floor (a mother appreciates this advantage).

Keeping a diverse selection of shower curtains on hand can change the bathroom in a matter of minutes. Ask your children what they would like in their bathroom. If you have a big football fan in the house, find fabric with their favorite football team on it. A bathroom is personal and whoever uses the room needs to be consulted.

There are so many fabric choices that you'll be able to customize it to suit anyone. Use decorator cotton prints, solids, or stripes. Or consider using white terrycloth, eyelet, pre-gathered ruffles, lace, and ribbon. Give your bathroom a new look with the latest mildew-resistant, laminated fabrics.

Tip

If using laminated fabric, use paper clips instead of pins to hold a seam. When sewing on the machine, place a sheet of tissue paper under the fabric. Hang the fabric with a shower liner.

A standard shower curtain is 72" x 72". If you use 45" or 54" wide fabric, you'll need 4½ yds. of a solid print or 4½ yds. plus one pattern repeat for a print shower curtain.

Materials:

❋ Fabric (45" or wider): 4½ yds.
Note: If using waterproof fabric, you won't need a liner. If not, purchase a liner to hang facing the water.
❋ Thread to match

Instructions:

1. Cut the fabric into 80" lengths. The extra 8" are for a double 1" top hem and a double 3" bottom hem.
2. With right sides together, sew the panels together with a 1/2" seam allowance. Match the pattern if you have one. Press the seam open.
3. Turn the side edges under 1/2" and 1/2" again. Stitch.
4. Turn the top edge down 1" and 1" again. Stitch.
5. Turn up the bottom edge 3" and 3" again. Stitch.

Tip

Drapery weights are a great idea in the bottom hem to keep the shower curtain outside the tub.

6. Add buttonholes, starting 1" from each end and at 5½" intervals. (Or use your purchased shower liner as a guide to mark buttonhole placement.) Make sure the buttonholes are vertical. If you don't want to make buttonholes, use easy-to-secure grommets to reinforce holes punched in the fabric.

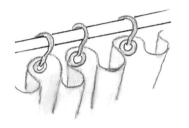

BRIGHT IDEAS FOR
SHOWER CURTAINS

❧ Use a jazzy animal print as a border for a single flounce.

❧ Use ties or tabs to hang the curtain instead of traditional hooks.

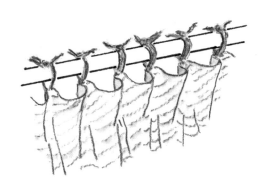

ties

tabs

When making a shower curtain with sewn tabs or ties, allow 1½ to two times the fullness. Double a 4″ bottom hem and double 1½″ side hems.

straight tabs

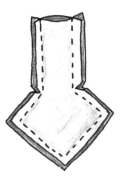 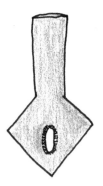 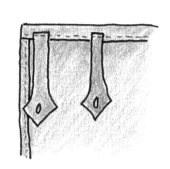 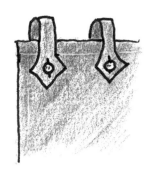

arrow tabs

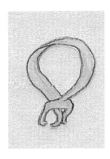 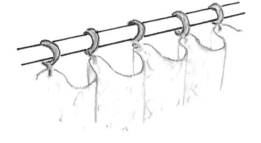

❀ The most common way to hang a shower curtain is to use shower curtain rings through the buttonholes.

❀ Make shirred tabs.

A single flounce with Battenberg lace.

❀ Fold over an attached flounce with buttonholes.

BRIGHT IDEAS
FOR BATHROOM ACCENTS

- ❧ Choose an unusual mirror above the sink or as an accent.
- ❧ Incorporate some small sculptures or collectibles.
- ❧ Stack fluffy towels in a basket.
- ❧ Put lotions and perfumes in decorative containers.
- ❧ Update the accessories - tissue cover, toothbrush holder, glass, etc.
- ❧ Work with bright and bold colors, using two main colors more than once in the room.
- ❧ If you don't want to rely on accessories to create interest, use a more dramatic color scheme on the walls.
- ❧ If the bathroom is small, stay away from decorating themes.
- ❧ Place containers in the bathroom that will keep clutter to a minimum.
- ❧ Add candles, lamps, plants, and photos.
- ❧ If you have a large room, add a small sofa and an unexpected rug.

Bathroom decor doesn't have to just include a sink and a soap dish. Try placing a special lamp and framed pictures to add warmth to this often sterile-looking environment.

If you have the room, it is a great plan to make a seating area in the bathroom along with your closet nearby. Create a theme such as oriental or something wild and crazy.

USING TOWELS
AS DECORATIVE ACCENTS

Perk up your bathroom by adding embellishments to inexpensive plain towels. Add lace, borders, monograms, embroidery, appliqué, or other decorative touches. Choose colors that will coordinate with the window treatments, shower curtain, or other special items in the bathroom.

Tip

When sewing any trims on terrycloth towels, use a longer stitch length on your machine.

If you have an animal theme throughout the house, you might want to carry the theme in to the bathroom. Adding animal prints on the edges of the towels or shower curtain completes the look.

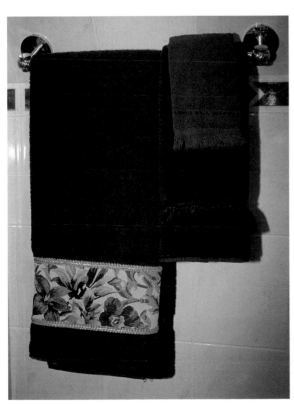

One towel rack doesn't necessarily mean one towel. Jazz it up a little by adding a variety of colors and sizes of towels. Even go so far as to add a border trim.

ADDING MACHINE EMBROIDERY
ON TOWELS

With the wide variety of machine embroidery designs available, you're sure to find something just right for your bathroom.

Materials:

❈ Towel
❈ Sticky stabilizer
❈ Machine hoop
❈ Dissolvable plastic film
❈ Contrasting thread

Instructions:

1. Place sticky stabilizer in your sewing machine hoop, then place the area of the towel to be stitched over the stabilizer. Press to secure.

2. Place a dissolvable plastic film over the towel. This will keep the terry loops from sagging or showing through the stitching. Stitch the embroidery design.

3. When finished, spritz off the plastic film. You will love the results.

MAKING A SINK/
DRESSING TABLE SKIRT

Older homes often have wall-mounted sinks that leave the plumbing exposed. A simple skirt around the sink could be the answer. You can also make a skirt for a dressing table.

A skirt made from brocade fabric edged with bullion fringe.

Materials:

❈ Fabric (45″ or wider): 4 yds. *Note:* This is an estimate. To determine the exact amount of fabric, measure the length from the top of the sink to the floor and add 2″. Measure the total circumference of the sink.

❈ Shirring tape (two or four cord): double the measurement around the upper edge of the sink

❈ Velcro with adhesive backing

❈ Thread to match

Instructions:

1. Cut a piece of fabric twice the circumference of the sink. The width should be the length from the sink to the floor plus 2″.

2. Cut a piece of shirring tape the same length.

3. Stitch the shirring tape along the length of the fabric with right sides together. Turn the tape to the wrong side and press.

4. With the shirring tape in one hand and the shirring cords in the other, begin gathering the fabric by pulling the cords. Gather the fabric evenly. Secure the cords when the gathers are evenly distributed.

5. Press the adhesive Velcro (hook side) on the top of the sink. The other piece (loop side) of Velcro will go on the skirt itself after it has been gathered. You might prefer to use nonstick Velcro so you can sew it on the top edge.

Tip

You can also make a skirt with a casing and put it on a spring rod.

The ultimate goal for your bathroom is a place where you can soak away all the cares of the world. It is a place where your day ends, but also begins - Alpha and Omega - a must for any beautiful home.

Bubbles fill spaces.

CHAPTER FIFTEEN

Around the Table – The Ultimate Gathering Place

The linen overhang adds a special touch to this kitchen counter.

THE HEART OF MOST HOMES IS THE KITCHEN. A KITCHEN CAN EITHER MATCH OR CONTRAST WITH THE REST OF THE HOUSE. EVEN IF YOU HAVE A HUGE GREAT ROOM (OR LIVING ROOM) THE MAJORITY OF VISITORS WILL END UP HANGING AROUND THE KITCHEN COUNTER. NO MATTER WHERE YOU SERVE YOUR GUESTS, THEY WILL INEVITABLY BE UNDER YOUR FEET IN THE KITCHEN. A KITCHEN IS A WORK AREA BUT IT IS ALSO A PLACE FOR MANY GOOD CONVERSATIONS. SPECIAL THOUGHT NEEDS TO BE TAKEN WHEN DECORATING THIS ULTIMATE GATHERING PLACE.

MANY KITCHENS ARE NOW FEATURING SPACE FOR A BREAKFAST AREA OR A COUNTER AND STOOLS. THIS IS A WONDERFUL SPOT TO HAVE THAT FIRST CUP OF COFFEE IN THE MORNING AND READ THE PAPER. WHAT BETTER WAY TO GET THE DAY STARTED OFF ON THE RIGHT FOOT?

MAKING CHAIR PADS

Since we have a tendency to sit awhile at the table, it is important to make the chairs as comfortable as possible. A cushion not only adds comfort, but brightens up the room.

The fabric on the chairs matches the design on the walls.

The chart below shows yardage requirements for many sizes of cushions, from chair size to sofa size.

Foam Thickness	Yards (54″ wide)		
	1″ to 1½″	2″	3″ to 4″
18″ x 18″	1	1½	
18″ x 24″	1¼	1½	
18″ x 36″	1½	1½	
18″ x 48″	1¾	2½	
18″ x 60″	2¼	2¾	
18″ x 72″	2½	3	
24″ x 24″			3
24″ x 36″			2½
24″ x 48″			3½
24″ x 60″			3½
24″ x 72″			4¼

Instructions:

1. Make a paper pattern of the chair seat. Cut two, adding a 1/2″ for seam allowance. Cut four ties 22″ long x 2½″ wide.

2. Fold the ties in half lengthwise, right sides together, and stitch all but one short end using a 1/2″ seam allowance.

Materials:

To make one cushion

✳ Fabric: 1⅝ yds. 45″ wide; 1½ yds. 54″ wide
✳ Polyester fiberfill or pillow form
✳ Thread to match

3. Turn the ties right side out and press. (Use a Fasturn tool if possible or a good old fashioned safety pin.)

4. With right sides together, pin two ties to each back corner of the seat cushion fabric.

5. With right sides together, place the other piece of seat cushion fabric over the first with the ties between.

6. Stitch, leaving an opening for turning and stuffing. Clip the curves and turn right side out.

7. Stuff with fiberfill or the pillow form. Turn under the opened edge and whipstitch or slipstitch it closed.

MAKING A ROUND TABLECLOTH

You can really tie a room together with tablecloths. Don't feel you are limited to one tablecloth, or two or three for that matter. You can make the topper shorter than the first one and a third one even shorter. Add lace or a ruffle of contrasting colors and you have created a great place to spend part of your busy day.

A wonderful place to sit and have your afternoon cup of tea. This table is covered with three cloths, each a different fabric. The two toppers are square and the floor length one is round.

Materials:

For a round tablecloth with 10″ drop

❃ Fabric (54″ wide):

    30″ finished diameter 1½ yds.

    36″ finished diameter 3¼ yds.

    48″ finished diameter 4 yds.

    54″ finished diameter 4¼ yds.

    60″ finished diameter 4½ yds.

    66″ finished diameter 5 yds.

Note: Allow extra to match a repeat pattern

❃ Thread to match

For a round tablecloth with a 30″ drop (shown)

❃ Fabric (54″ wide):

    30″ finished diameter 5 yds.

    36″ finished diameter 5½ yds.

    48″ finished diameter 6 yds.

    54″ finished diameter 9½ yds.

    60″ finished diameter 10 yds.

    66″ finished diameter 10½ yds.

    72″ finished diameter 11 yds.

Note: Allow extra to match a repeat pattern

❃ Thread to match

Instructions:

1. Depending on the width of the fabric, you may have to piece the fabric together or cut a one-piece circle. If your cut length is greater than the width of your fabric, you will need to purchase two or three lengths of fabric and piece together as shown. Refer to measuring directions in Chapter Six.

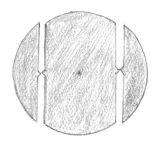

2. To cut a circle you need string, a fabric marker, and a tack or your thumb. Fold the fabric into fourths with the right side on the inside. Place a tack or your thumb at the corner fold and attach a string to a marker. Draw an arc across the fabric. (You might want to practice on paper first.)

Starting the circle.

Completing the circle.

3. A second method of sizing the fabric is to center the fabric on the table and anchor it with heavy books so the fabric won't shift during marking. The fabric should hang 8″ to 12″ from the tabletop or to the floor, plus 1/2″ for the hem allowance. Position the fabric so the straight of the grain goes lengthwise on the table.

4. Use a ruler and fabric marker to mark the drop from the tabletop (your desired length). Measure down from the top of the table and mark with chalk at the desired length as you go completely around the bottom edge of the fabric. Cut on these marks.

5. To finish the tablecloth edge, use a serger if you own one or stitch a 1/2″ hem on the sewing machine.

MAKING A SQUARE TABLE TOPPER

Materials:

To make a 54″ square topper
- ❀ Fabric (54″ wide): 1½ yds.
- ❀ Tassels: 4
- ❀ Fringe: 6 yds.
- ❀ Thread to match

Instructions:

1. Lay the fabric on the table, making sure the grainline is straight on the horizontal line of the table. Cut a 54″ square of fabric.

2. Place the trim on the fabric with right sides together around all four edges and stitch.

3. Sew one tassel on each corner. Quick and easy!

Tip
Alternate Hem Finishes

- ❀ Turn the hem edge to the right side and cover with purchased braid, ball fringe, or single fold bias tape.
- ❀ Finish the raw edge with a three-step zigzag stitch.

MAKING TABLE RUNNERS/PLACE MATS

Making table runners, place mats, and napkins are a quick way to change the look in your kitchen. If you are not crazy about sewing but enjoy the end result, these quick and easy-to-sew table accessories are for you. They are also excellent for gift giving.

For table runners, your table shape and personal preference will dictate your needs. A long narrow table might have two runners placed lengthwise. Or use two runners crosswise to seat four; center a third runner on the table length to seat six. A round or oblong table might have two runners placed at right angles. Or top a tablecloth with a quilted runner to serve as decorative protection from hot dishes.

Single face quilted fabric, linen-like weaves, and decorator prints are excellent fabric options. Consider the less traditional fabrics too. Natural canvas, for example, trimmed with navy might better suit a summer picnic table or beach front condominium. A contemporary glass and chrome décor might call for a taupe suede cloth.

To add interest, use a contrasting lining - back a beige and tan seashell print with a coordinating solid tan. For a white linen-like fabric, use a self-lining and pale blue cording to accent fragile silver-trimmed china. For a country table setting, use a tiny navy/white provincial print, backed with navy and piped in red.

A finished table runner should be 12″ to 15″ wide, depending on the table size. For a good balance, the longer the table, the wider the runner. The length hanging over the table edge should be 8″ to 10″. If you want to add length, do it at both ends. For example, add two 12″ lengths to a 24″ panel to equal 48″ rather than joining a 36″ length and a 12″ length.

Place mats are typically 14″ x 18″. Whether you're making runners or place mats, the instructions are the same - just the size changes.

Method #1

For lightweight fabric where two thicknesses will be used, cord the seams. Use narrow seam allowances - about 1/4″ or the width of the cording seam allowance. Seams will need no trimming and the bonus will be fabric edges that pull out easily just by turning the runner and pushing the cording away from the seams with a steam iron.

Materials:

❀ Fabric: 1⅞ yds. to 2¾ yds. (depending on length of runner)
❀ Fleece: 2¾ yds.
❀ Thread to match
❀ Tassels: 2

Instructions:

1. Cut two pieces of fabric to size, plus 1/2″ longer and 1/2″ wider. Cut a piece of fleece the size of the fabric, less 1/2″ on all sides. Baste the fleece to the wrong side of one fabric piece.

2. Stitch cording to the right side of the fleece-backed fabric piece. Place the two fabric pieces right sides together and insert tassels at the ends.

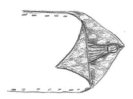

3. Pin and stitch around the entire runner or mat, leaving an opening for turning. Stitch precisely on the first row of stitching.
4. Turn right side out and close the opening with a whipstitch, slipstitch, or fusible web.

Method #2

Use this method for heavy fabric such as canvas, suede cloth, or decorator fabric that requires no lining.

Materials:

❀ Fabric: 1⅞ yds. to 2¾ yds. (depending on length of runner)
❀ Thread to match
❀ Tassels: 2

Instructions:

1. Cut one runner or mat to size, adding 2½″ to the width and 1″ to the length for hemming.
2. Finish all the raw edges with a zigzag stitch or serge the edge.

3. Fold a 1″ hem to the wrong side along both long edges and pin.
4. *Optional:* With the hem pinned in place and working on the right side, add a trim such as a wide bias tape. If the trim is so wide that two rows of stitching are required, be sure to stitch each side in the same direction to avoid puckering.
5. Machine topstitch, making sure these stitches are as straight as possible.

Tip

Use a decorative machine stitch for the topstitching. Or use a contrasting thread.

MAKING NAPKINS

Red and gold linen napkins spice up the kitchen table.

Materials:

❀ Fabric: amount depends on the size napkins you want. 16″ is considered dinner size and 12″ is considered lunch size. One yd. of 45″ wide fabric will make four dinner napkins or six luncheon napkins.

❀ Thread to match

Instructions

1. Cut the fabric to size plus 1/2″.

2. Stitch 1/2″ around all four sides

3. On the corner, trim off the point to reduce the bulk.

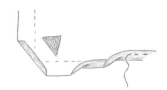

4. Fold over 1/4″ and 1/4″ again and stitch down.

Option: Use a rolled-hem stitch on your serger for a quick and easy finish.

KITCHEN WINDOW TREATMENTS

These Roman shades can be functional or mock. Refer to Chapter Twelve for making directions.

This decorative shade doesn't go up or down and the valance is actually wood that has been painted.

Window treatments are also important when decorating your kitchen. Before you choose a style, consider the following:

❀ How much light do you want in your kitchen?

❀ Do you like the view?

❀ Are you concerned with privacy?

❀ What will the window treatments look like from the outside?

❀ Will you open the window?

❀ Does the kitchen window treatment have to match the rest of the house?

Friends and guests fill kitchens.

CHAPTER SIXTEEN

Special Places at Home or On the Go

Hallways, window seats, lofts, attics, porches, corners, and yes, even your pet area, can all present a decorating nightmare. These tight corners have always been a decorating dilemma but there are ways to resolve them. When working in a very small area, pay attention to lighting. Use wall coverings to add warmth and try new textures. Remember that sewing for the home is fun and highly satisfying and can certainly save you a bundle of money. As you approach these special areas, remember to include in your cost factor the paint, drapery hardware, carpeting or rugs, and lighting. Even with those extras added, you will still be way ahead of the game by doing it yourself.

HALLS & ENTRANCES

The hallway is a perfect place to put various items such as a bench, pillows, sporting items, a small table with a special vase and a family picture. Recently I looked at my long hallway and realized it was bare. I gathered up all my framed pictures - the ones that were in closets because I didn't know where to hang them - and started hanging them on the wall. The frames are all different but after completing the task, I stood back and shouted for joy. We call it our "Cowan Hall of Fame" and all the children, grandchildren, grandparents, and friends feel very honored to be hung in our hall.

An entranceway is another question mark when decorating. There usually isn't much room here, but to leave it bare is to "leave it bare." The number one goal is to make the entranceway a welcoming center. This small area actually symbolizes how the world sees you. For some visitors, like the mailman, it might be the only area he sees. What message do you want people to gather from this tiny area? Think about adding a small seat, a table with flowers, or a table with your favorite figurines. These items should whet the appetite for guests to want to see the rest of your home.

Top Right: This hallway leading to the master bedroom features a bench with two bows on each end.

Right: This antique table in the hallway offers insight to the homeowner's taste and interests.

LOFTS & ATTICS

A loft or attic usually has slanted ceilings. These in themselves cause the best decorator to scratch his or her head. A simple swag draped around an odd size window just might do the trick. Depending on the size of the area, you could add a dressing table or a chest of drawers. Don't forget to add your personal pictures to give it that feeling of home.

An attic or a loft can also include small or odd shaped windows. If you need the light, leave the window uncovered, but decorate it with a few small trinkets or figurines on the sill.

Above Left: An attic doesn't have to look dark or neglected. This gathered lace panel framed with a cascading swag makes the area inviting.

Left: The ungathered lace panel in the attic was part of the train on a wedding veil.

Above: Even though there's no window covering, this window doesn't look bare.

CORNERS

A corner can mean different things to different people. It can mean a place to rock your baby to sleep, a place to dream and scheme, or a place to sit down while putting on your shoes.

Often a corner can be filled with a small table draped with a brightly colored tablecloth or with a beautiful screen and a potted plant. If the corner is otherwise okay, add a tall shelf to put various items on such as teapots, vases, or canisters.

Above: This interlined, lined jumbo welted table skirt was made from fabric from France. The damask striped cover adds a special touch.

Right: Placing a comfortable chair in a corner converts it into usable space.

PORCHES

If your decorating dilemma area happens to be the front porch, you might consider a porch swing. Keep in mind the fabrics should be weather-oriented and don't be afraid to throw on lots of pillows of various sizes and shapes.

If you often spend time waiting at the back door for children or other loved ones, add a wooden bench with a magazine rack. Cover the pad to match your interior and you won't mind waiting so much. Whether making a pad for a bench or one for a kitchen chair, it is very similar. Just the size changes.

Top Left: What could be more inviting than a porch swing covered with an attractive cushion and pillows?

Middle Left: Perfect for warm summer nights, everyone will enjoy sitting on the porch in this wicker sofa.

Below Left: Place a magazine rack and a bench near the back door for those times when you end up waiting for someone to get ready to go.

PET PROJECTS FOR THE "OTHER MEMBER OF THE FAMILY"

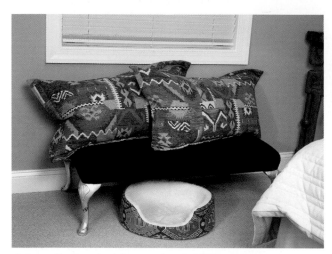

A fleece-lined cat bed that matches the decor.

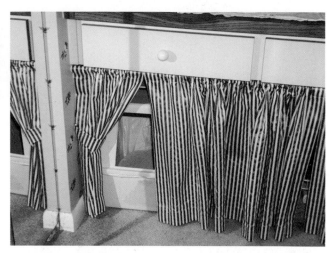

The simple gathered drape on a spring rod camouflages the litter box.

If your dog has royalty in its blood, add a swag tied with rope cording and throw in a pillow and lots of bones. This is what you call "top dog."

Use washable fabrics in areas where the animals like to nap.

You don't have to give up style and beauty to include your favorite pet in the home decorating scheme. After all, a house is not a home without your pet. Dogs and cats love to hide and burrow themselves. So with that in mind, include the pet in your decision making. How about a pet bed made from fabric that matches your bedspread?

Another good idea is covering an out of the way area with a fabric drape to allow your cat some privacy and to keep the litter box out of sight. That's how I solved our kitty litter box

problem. Just inside our back door is a closet door with slats. I took out the bottom ten slats and put the litter box inside the closet. The cat has privacy and I don't have to trip around the litter box in my bathroom.

Cats love to sit in the window. If you are planning to add a windowsill extension, consider covering it with matching or coordinating carpet. A scratching post doesn't need to stick out like a sore thumb. If you make your own, cover it with carpet that complements the colors in your room. Even purchased scratching posts

come in a variety of colors.

There are so many animal prints to decorate with, so go look and have fun in the fabric store. Your dog's favorite pillow can be covered with an animal print pillowcase. Home decorating should be a family affair but it might be a problem if you take your pet with you to the fabric store to pick out the fabric of choice.

Anyone who owns a pet knows the bottom line is this: Your pet will sleep anywhere it wants to. Even if you insist otherwise, eventually the pet will wear you down.

THE HOME OFFICE

Nooks and crannies are not the only special places in your home that cause a home decorator to think twice. Special areas also include offices at home.

The sign of the times is an office at home. No more escaping work at home. I personally prefer it this way and love the fact that I can sew and write at home and put a pot roast in the oven for dinner and never miss a beat. Having my office at home affords very flexible hours, a short commute to my office (a flight of stairs), and a cat at my feet. This is the best of both worlds.

Your work area at home needs to project that feeling of comfort and put any visitors or clients at ease. It needs to say "Welcome." If sharing the space, then decisions need to be made with that other person in mind. Remember to avoid clutter so your clients won't feel they have to move a mountain of stuff to sit down. If clients will be waiting at times, and you have enough room, add a small sofa and chair. Be sure to keep a nice selection of current magazines on hand.

Your work area at home also needs to be a place where you can avoid the hustle-and-bustle of everyday life. Surround yourself with items that tell a visitor what you are all about. This is a place where you create - a place that keeps you sane. If you have a desk, think of it as a map of your life. Keep your desk clean and clear of clutter so you have more room to let the creative juices run.

If the walls are primarily of dark wood, consider letting in as much light as possible. On the door or window, use shirred curtains. Mount them on either a single rod pole or spring rods - simple but effective.

Above: The waiting area in this home office is welcoming and comfortable.

Bottom: Any office, at home or otherwise, should be light and airy. The small windows above the sheers let in even more light. You really can have your cake and eat it too.

Let your individual style dictate the look of your home office. Rick Bryant chose to make a cornice board with banners edged in rope cording for his office.

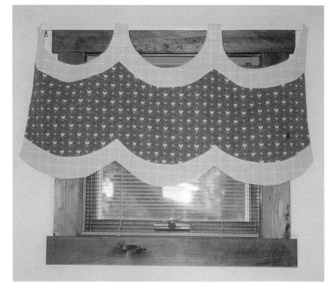

The window coverings in my home office make it a fun place to work and entertain clients. See Chapter Twelve for instructions on making the cornice board and valance.

When deciding what space to convert into an office, consider a spare bedroom, under the eaves of an attic, a former laundry room, or a small building in your backyard (not the doghouse). Not all offices in a home have to be for work only. Many people include an entertainment center so the room can do double duty during off hours. No matter where you have your office, it should be a place where dreams come true - in my case, one stitch at a time.

My offices consist of a sewing room and a computer room. I am fortunate to have separate rooms, so I treat them differently. My sewing room is filled with subtle colors and lots of fluorescent lighting and my office is fun and cheerful. While writing this book I added a custom valance on a cornice board and a matching stool cover in my office. Outside the office I have a smaller window where I have a small desk to write notes and checks and a stool where I sit. I gave that window treatment a scalloped edge, rather than a straight edge.

MAKING AN OFFICE STOOL COVER

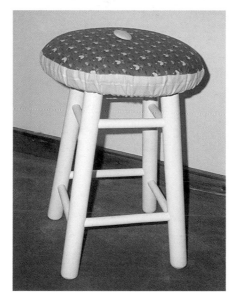

It's so handy to have a stool or two in the office. I covered mine with fabric to coordinate with the window treatments.

Materials:

* Fabric:
    1/2 yd. for the stool cover
    1/2 yd. contrasting fabric
        for the boxing strip
* Lining: 1/2 yd.
* Batting: 1/2 yd.
* Thread to match
* Elastic or string

Instructions:

1. If the stool top is already covered, remove the old cover and use it as a pattern. If it's not covered, make a paper pattern. Cut fabric, lining, and batting to fit, adding a 1/2″ seam allowance to the fabric and lining, but not the batting.

2. Cut a boxing strip of contrasting fabric the depth and circumference of the stool plus 1″.

3. Make a sandwich of the fabric, batting, and lining. Stitch the three layers together.

4. With right sides together, sew the short ends of the boxing strip together. Mark quarters on the fabric/batting/lining circle and pin the boxing strip to the circle with right sides together. Be sure to position the boxing strip evenly around the circle. Stitch.

5. Turn 1/2″ under on the outside edge of the boxing strip and stitch a casing. Insert a length of elastic or a drawstring

6. If desired, sew on a covered button. Refer to Chapter Nine for instructions on covering the button. Use a double thread to secure the button in the center through all layers. If you sit on this stool often, you might want to consider leaving off the button - for obvious reasons.

7. Place the cover on the stool and pull the elastic or drawstring tight and secure with a knot.

MAKING A
COMPUTER MONITOR COVER

It's a rare office that doesn't include a computer. A computer monitor cover can add a special touch to the office. After you have made the monitor cover, consider covering the keyboard and perhaps, even the mouse! Monitors come in different sizes and shapes, so this cover is easy to adapt to your monitor.

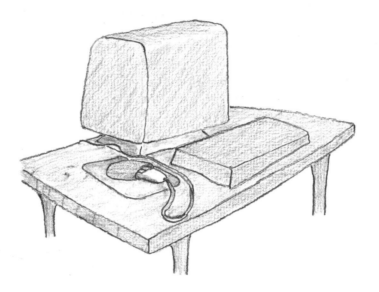

Materials:

To make a cover for a 17″ monitor:
* Fabric (54″ wide): 1½ yds.
* Thread to match

Instructions:

1. Cut a piece of fabric that will completely cover the monitor, front, back, and sides.

2. Drape the fabric over the monitor wrong side out. Pin the corners as shown, keeping the pins vertical.

3. Use a chalk marker to mark the pin placements, then remove the pins and sew along these marks. Trim away the excess fabric.

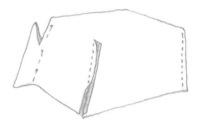

4. Hem the bottom raw edge by turning up 1/2″ and stitch. Or use your serger.

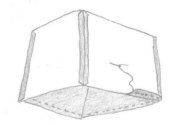

A HOME ON WHEELS

Perhaps you want to take your home on the road. Some people call them RVs, some call them campers, and some call them buses, but all call them home. If you've made the investment, chances are you're going to spend a great deal of time within these mobile walls. You can make this environment as homey as any stationary building by adding personal touches and bringing along some special items that have meaning to you.

Above Left: This cozy living room is decorated with a flower print sofa and many pillows of contrasting fabric. Some pillows are wrapped with heavy cord and others are fastened in the middle with a button.

Left: In the bathroom, the fringed hand towels feature a contrasting band sewn on the bottom of each towel.

Postscript

Tools fill spaces, colors fill spaces, fabrics fill spaces, inches fill spaces, stitches fill spaces, style fills spaces, pillows fill spaces, curtains fill spaces, children fill spaces, loved ones fill spaces, pets fill spaces, friends fill spaces, bubbles fill spaces, and guests fill spaces. Ultimately these spaces are tied together with the sheer desire to make your house a home. I hope this journey was worth every minute and your own personal spaces are now all full.

Remember to sew the times of your life with love.

About the Author

TELEVISION PERSONALITY, SEWING EXPERT, AUTHOR, SYNDICATED COLUMNIST, MOTIVATIONAL SPEAKER, WIFE, STEPMOTHER, AND MENTOR ALL DESCRIBE SALLY COWAN. SHE IS AN INSPIRING AND MOTIVATING INDIVIDUAL WHO CAPTURES HER AUDIENCES WITH HER REMARKABLE HUMOR. HER GOAL IS TO THOROUGHLY "KEEP YOU IN STITCHES."

TO SALLY, *KEEPING YOU IN STITCHES* IS MORE THAN THE TITLE OF HER SUCCESSFUL SEWING AND LECTURE SERIES, IT IS THE PHILOSOPHY ON WHICH SHE HAS BASED HER LIFE. SALLY'S MISSION IS TO TREAT EACH PERSON AS AN INDIVIDUAL WITH SPECIAL TALENTS TO BE USED AS STEPPING STONES, NOT STUMBLING BLOCKS.

"NO MATTER WHAT ADJUSTMENTS HAVE TO BE TAKEN AT THE SEWING MACHINE, THE IMPORTANCE OF AN ACCOMPLISHMENT BY EACH INDIVIDUAL IS WHAT MATTERS THE MOST," SAYS SALLY.

SALLY DEVELOPED HER LOVE OF SEWING AS A CHILD, UNDER THE WATCHFUL EYE OF HER GRANDMOTHER. BEFORE LONG, SHE WAS SHARING HER KNOWLEDGE OF SEWING WITH OTHERS. AN OFFHAND SUGGESTION BY ONE OF HER NURSING INSTRUCTORS CONVINCED SALLY THAT SHE SHOULD COMBINE HER SEWING KNOWLEDGE, SENSE OF HUMOR, AND CREATIVE TEACHING STYLE AND GAVE BIRTH TO THE CONCEPT FOR *KEEPING YOU IN STITCHES*.

SALLY IS THE AUTHOR OF *LEFT-HANDED SEWING, LEFT-HANDED STITCHERY, CELEBRATE WITH KEEPING YOU IN STITCHES,* AND *KEEPING YOU IN STITCHES 100*.

SALLY TRAVELS THROUGHOUT THE UNITED STATES AND CANADA PRESENTING PROGRAMS ON TOPICS SUCH AS HEALTH AND WELL BEING, SEWING, AND MOTIVATION. HER FUNDAMENTAL APPROACH TO LEARNING IS THAT DISABILITIES (WHETHER REAL OR PERCEIVED) ARE NOT OBSTACLES, BUT CHALLENGES TO BE OVERCOME WITH HUMOR AND A POSITIVE ATTITUDE.

Home Decorating Websites

www.kyistitches.com
www.housenet.com
www.homeworkers.org/iha.htm
www.sherwinwilliams.com/diy
www.sewstorm.com
www.livinghome.com
www.monogramit.com
www.nariorg
www.eta.mfi.com
www.apartmentlife.com
www.supersilk.com
www.remodeling.hw.net
www.fabricclub.com
www.benjaminmoore.com
www.diy.co.uk/howto.htm
www.homebase.com/home.html
www.garden.com
www.amazon.co.uk
www.lonelyplanet.co.uk
www.last-minute.co.uk
www.mondadori.com/interni
www.sewing.org/home.html
www.ssew.com
www.cmc-one.com/elegant/index
www.myinteriordecorator.com
www.decoratingsecrets.com
www.homearts.com
www.sampler.com
www.m'fay.com

Original Decor You Can Create with Ease

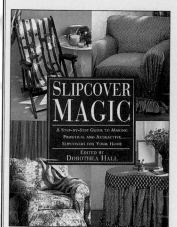

Slipcover Magic
by Dorothea Hall and Ron Carolissen
From formal fitted to loose no-sew, the slipcover designs in this book are shown in lovely watercolor illustrations and full-color photographs. Includes instructions for you to easily fashion sofa and armchair treatments, upright chair covers, bedrooms and boudoirs, and much more.

Softcover • 8-1/4 x 10-7/8
• 128 pages
color throughout
SLMA • $21.95

Fabulous Floorcloths
Create Contemporary Floor Coverings from an Old World Art
by Caroline O'Neill Kuchinsky
Contemporary or antique, a canvas floorcloth transforms an ordinary floor into a work of art. Step-by-step instructions guide you through projects easily. Designs and color schemes for 14 projects from simple to advanced.

Softcover • 8-1/4 x 10-7/8
• 128 pages
60 color photos
• 225 color diagrams
FLODEC • $19.95

Tassels, Tiebacks, & Trimmings and How to Use Them
by Elizabeth Valenti
Add a touch of class to your home decor with these 50+ creative ideas for using simple accents. Contains step by step instructions for creating unique accessories from ready-made tassels, as well as how-to instructions to make your own basic tassel.

Softcover • 8-1/2 x 11
• 128 pages
color throughout
TTTHQ • $19.95

How to Dress a Naked Window
by Donna Babylon
Open your windows to a whole new look! Create window treatments packed with personality. Put up hardware, match repeating patterns and make Roman shades, tabs, valances and more with easy-to-follow instructions. You also will learn about basic terms, techniques and supplies.

Softcover • 8-1/4 x 10-7/8
• 96 pages
color throughout
HDNW • $19.95

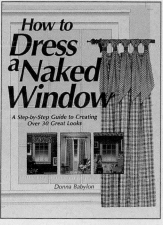

The Complete Step-by-Step Guide to Home Sewing
by Jeanne Argent
Lavishly illustrated with full-color photos, this book is packed with practical suggestions and clear, step-by-step diagrams that show you exactly how to make draperies, curtains and blinds, bed linens, table linens and even elegant, tailored lampshades.

Softcover • 8-1/4 x 10-7/8
• 240 pages
color throughout
CGHS • $24.95

Sew-It-Yourself Home Decor
Fabric Projects for the Living Room, Bedroom & Beyond
by Karen Coetzee and Rene Bergh
This beautiful book includes simple step-by-step instructions for more than 30 home dec projects including window treatments, bed covers, table linens, pillows, chair covers, and more. Also includes sewing techniques and simple measuring instructions.

Softcover • 8-1/2 x 11
• 160 pages
300 illustrations
• 200 color photos
SFUR • $21.95

Elegant Projects with Simple Techniques

Forever Flowers
A Flower Lover's Guide to Selecting, Pressing, and Designing
by Bernice Peitzer

Make your flowers last a lifetime! This all-in-one resource includes foolproof methods for sowing, growing, gathering, pressing, storing, and designing and creating with flowers. Provides dozens of projects and ideas for beautiful, functional accents you can keep yourself or give as one-of-a-kind gifts, including pictures, jewelry, bottles, and stationery. Features step-by-step instructions, lavish full-color photos, and tried-and-true tips and techniques.

Softcover • 8-1/4 x 10-7/8 • 128 pages
100 color photos
PRFLO • $21.95

Crafting Lamps & Shades
Easy, Inexpensive and Unique Projects To Light Up Your Home
by Jodie Davis

No matter what decorating style you prefer, from country or contemporary to sweet or sensational, one of the 30 lamp and shade projects in this book will turn boring into beautiful in just a few hours of fun. Easy-to-follow step-by-step instructions and illustrations demystify the wiring process and help create a house full of imaginative lamps and shades.

Softcover • 8-1/4 x 10-7/8 • 144 pages
50 color photos and 150 illustrations
LASH • $21.95

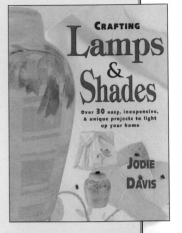

Sewing for your Garden
by Carolyn Vosburg Hall

If you love to sew and garden, this book is a must-have! You will find hours of enjoyment creating any of the 50 innovative, colorful, practical projects like tablecloths, totes, blankets, knee pads, gloves, aprons, centerpieces, and wind socks that will help you dig in the garden, serve lunch on the patio, frolic by the pool, or tailgate at the big game.

Softcover • 8-1/4 x 10-7/8 • 128 pages
90 color photos and 180 illustrations
SGAR • $19.95

Adventures with Polarfleece
A Sewing Expedition
by Nancy Cornwell

Nancy Cornwell will lead you on a sewing expedition. Explore and discover endless project possibilities for the entire family. Sew a collection of 15 projects for play, work, fashion, comfort and warmth. The heart of a fallen-away sewer will soon be recaptured and new sewers will be intrigued and inspired.

Softcover • 8-1/2 x 11
• 160 pages
200 color photos
150 color illustrations
AWPF • $19.95

All-New Instant Interiors
by Gail Brown

One hundred fast and simple projects help you decorate with fabric. Sew and no-sew shortcut techniques for table toppers, window treatments, bed covers, slipcovers, pillows and cushions, wall coverings and accessories.

Softcover • 8-1/4 x 10-7/8 • 96 pages
2 color throughout

More Polarfleece® Adventures
by Nancy Cornwell

Add designer touches to fleece with cutwork, sculpturing, appliqué, pintucking, fancy edge finishes, designer buttonholes, and machine embroidery. Start off with a quick refresher course and end with a chapter filled with fun fleece projects. In between, you'll find a new world pat-